Academic Encounters

2nd Edition

Yoneko Kanaoka
Series Editor: Bernard Seal

The Natural World 1

LISTENING

SPEAKING

CAMBRIDGE
UNIVERSITY PRESS

CAMBRIDGE
UNIVERSITY PRESS

University Printing House, Cambridge CB2 8BS, United Kingdom

One Liberty Plaza, 20th Floor, New York, NY 10006, USA

477 Williamstown Road, Port Melbourne, VIC 3207, Australia

4843/24, 2nd Floor, Ansari Road, Daryaganj, Delhi – 110002, India

79 Anson Road, #06–04/06, Singapore 079906

Cambridge University Press is part of the University of Cambridge.

It furthers the University's mission by disseminating knowledge in the pursuit of
education, learning and research at the highest international levels of excellence.

www.cambridge.org
Information on this title: www.cambridge.org/9781316995655

© Cambridge University Press 2013

First published 2007
Second edition 2013
20 19 18 17 16 15 14 13 12 11 10 9 8 7 6 5 4 3 2 1

Printed in the United Kingdom by Latimer Trend

A catalog record for this publication is available from the British Library

Library of Congress Cataloging in Publication Data

Kanaoka, Yoneko.
    Academic encounters : the natural world : listening, speaking. -- 2nd edition./ Yoneko Kanaoka.
        pages cm. -- (Academic encounters)
    Includes index.
    Previous edition: 2009, written by Wharton, Jennifer.
        ISBN 978-1-107-67463-9 (pbk. : level 1) -- ISBN 978-1-107-63825-9 (audio CDs› : level 1)
1. English language--Textbooks for foreign speakers. 2. English language--Rhetoric--Problems,
exercises, etc. 3. Study skills--Problems, exercises, etc. 4. Earth sciences--Problems, exercises, etc.
5. Readers (Secondary) I. Title.

PE1128.W57 2013
428.2'4--dc23

2013004917

ISBN 978-1-316-99565-5 Student's Book with Integrated Digital Learning
ISBN 978-1-107-64492-2 Teacher's Manual

Additional resources for this publication at www.cambridge.org/academicencounters

Art direction and layout services: Kamae Design, Oxford, UK
Photo research: Suzanne Williams
Audio production: John Marshall Media
Video production: Steadman Productions

Table of Contents

Scope and Sequence

Unit 1: Planet Earth • 1

	Content	Ⓛ Listening Skills	Ⓢ Speaking Skills
Chapter 1 **The Physical Earth** page 3	**Interview 1** A Geologist Talks **Interview 2** Earth's Natural Beauty **Lecture** A Look Inside Planet Earth	Listening to directions Listening for main ideas in an interview Listening for details Listening for main ideas in a lecture	Sharing your knowledge Sharing your opinion Discussing what you have learned
Chapter 2 **The Dynamic Earth** page 18	**Interview 1** Living Near an Active Volcano **Interview 2** Living with Earthquakes **Lecture** Volcanoes	Listening to numerical information about distances and rates Understanding multiple-choice questions Drawing inferences	Interpreting a map Responding to a speaker Retelling what you have heard Sharing ideas

Unit 2: Water on Earth • 41

	Content	Ⓛ Listening Skills	Ⓢ Speaking Skills
Chapter 3 **Earth's Water Supply** page 43	**Interview 1** Water in the United States **Interview 2** Water in Cambodia **Interview 3** Water in Africa **Lecture** Sources and Functions of Surface Water	Listening for opinions Listening for details Listening for specific information	Examining graphic material Examining a map Applying what you have learned Predicting the content Considering related information
Chapter 4 **Earth's Oceans** page 62	**Interview 1** Adventure Under the Ocean **Interview 2** Surf's Up **Lecture** One World Ocean	Expressing likes and dislikes Predicting the content Listening for main ideas Thinking critically about the topic Personalizing the topic Listening for signal words	Sharing your opinion Retelling what you have heard Thinking creatively about the topic Building background knowledge on the topic

V Vocabulary Skills	**N** Note Taking Skills	Learning Outcomes
Reading and thinking about the topic Understanding word parts Examining vocabulary in context Guessing vocabulary from context	Organizing your notes in an outline Listening for supporting details Clarifying your notes with a partner Using your notes to label an illustration	Prepare and deliver an oral presentation about a natural disaster
Reading and thinking about the topic Building background knowledge on the topic Guessing vocabulary from context Predicting the content	Focusing on the introduction Using telegraphic language Using your notes to make a study sheet	

V Vocabulary Skills	**N** Note Taking Skills	Learning Outcomes
Reading and thinking about the topic Building background vocabulary Guessing vocabulary from context	Using symbols and abbreviations Using bullets and brackets to organize your notes Rewriting your notes after a lecture	Prepare and deliver an oral presentation about daily water usage
Reading and thinking about the topic Guessing vocabulary from context	Using handouts to help you take notes Focusing on the conclusion Making test questions from your notes	

Unit 3: The Air Around Us • 83

	Content	Ⓛ Listening Skills	Ⓢ Speaking Skills
Chapter 5 **Earth's Atmosphere** page 85	**Interview 1** Pollutants in the Air **Interview 2** Air Quality **Interview 3** Humid and Dry Air **Lecture** What Is In the Air Out There?	Listening for background noise Listening for specific information Answering multiple-choice questions	Examining a map Sharing your experience Conducting an experiment Predicting the content Applying what you have learned
Chapter 6 **Weather and Climate** page 102	**Interview 1** A Future Meteorologist **Interview 2** Severe Weather **Lecture** Global Warming	Listening for specific information Predicting the content Listening for opinions Listening for numerical information Listening for cause and effect	Personalizing the topic Understanding humor about the topic Thinking critically about the topic Applying what you have learned

Unit 4: Life on Earth • 123

	Content	Ⓛ Listening Skills	Ⓢ Speaking Skills
Chapter 7 **Plants and Animals** page 125	**Interview 1** A Green Thumb **Interview 2** The Galapagos Islands **Lecture** What Is a Living Thing?	Listening for specific information Listening for examples Listening for expressions of contrast	Personalizing the topic Building background knowledge on the topic Examining graphic material Thinking critically about the topic Conducting an interview Applying what you have learned
Chapter 8 **Humans** page 142	**Interview 1** Running Track **Interview 2** Eat to Live, Don't Live to Eat **Lecture** Systems of the Human Body	Listening to directions Listening for main ideas Listening for specific information Listening for expressions of time order	Personalizing the topic Building background knowledge on the topic Conducting a survey Considering related information Sharing your opinion

V Vocabulary Skills	N Note Taking Skills	Learning Outcomes
Reading and thinking about the topic Building background knowledge and vocabulary Examining vocabulary in context Identifying key vocabulary in the lecture Guessing vocabulary from context	Organizing your notes in an outline Organizing your notes in a chart	Prepare and deliver an oral presentation about global warming with a partner
Reading and thinking about the topic Understanding scientific symbols Examining vocabulary in context Building background knowledge on the topic Guessing vocabulary from context	Copying a lecturer's illustrations	

V Vocabulary Skills	N Note Taking Skills	Learning Outcomes
Reading and thinking about the topic Examining vocabulary in context Previewing the topic Guessing vocabulary from context	Checking your notes Organizing your notes in a chart	Prepare and deliver an oral presentation about a living thing in Earth's biosphere
Reading and thinking about the topic Examining vocabulary in context Building background knowledge on the topic Guessing vocabulary from context	Taking notes in a flowchart Evaluating your own note-taking	

Academic Encounters: Academic Preparation Through Sustained Content

The Series

Academic Encounters is a sustained content-based series for English language learners preparing to study college-level subject matter in English. The goal of the series is to expose students to the types of texts and tasks that they will encounter in their academic course work and provide them with the skills to be successful when that encounter occurs.

Academic Content

At each level in the series, there are two thematically paired books. One is an academic reading and writing skills book, in which students encounter readings that are based on authentic academic texts. In this book, students are given the skills to understand texts and respond to them in writing. The reading and writing book is paired with an academic listening and speaking skills book, in which students encounter discussion and lecture material specially prepared by experts in their field. In this book, students learn how to take notes from a lecture, participate in discussions, and prepare short presentations.

Flexibility

The books at each level may be used as stand-alone reading and writing books or listening and speaking books. They may also be used together to create a complete four-skills course. This is made possible because the content of each book at each level is very closely related. Each unit and chapter, for example, has the same title and deals with similar content, so that teachers can easily focus on different skills, but the same content, as they toggle from one book to the other. Additionally, if the books are taught together, when students are presented with the culminating unit writing or speaking assignment, they will have a rich and varied supply of reading and lecture material to draw on.

A Sustained Content Approach

A sustained content approach teaches language through the study of subject matter from one or two related academic content areas. This approach simulates the experience of university courses and better prepares students for academic study.

Students benefit from a sustained content approach

Real-world academic language and skills
Students learn how to understand and use academic language because they are studying actual academic content.

An authentic, intensive experience
By immersing students in the language of a single academic discipline, sustained content helps prepare them for the rigor of later coursework.

Natural recycling of language
Because a sustained content course focuses on a particular academic discipline, concepts and language recur. As students progress through the course, their ability to work with authentic language improves dramatically.

Knowledge of common academic content
When students work with content from the most popular university courses, they gain real knowledge of these academic disciplines. This helps them to be more successful when they move on to later coursework.

The Content Areas of *Academic Encounters*

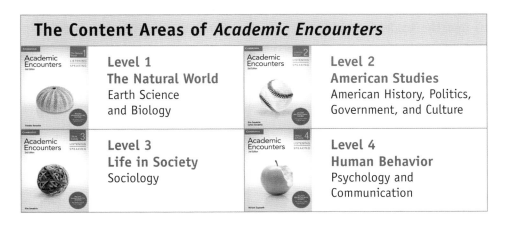

Level 1
The Natural World
Earth Science and Biology

Level 2
American Studies
American History, Politics, Government, and Culture

Level 3
Life in Society
Sociology

Level 4
Human Behavior
Psychology and Communication

Academic Skills

Academic Encounters, Listening and Speaking teaches skills in 4 main areas. A set of icons highlights which skills are practiced in each exercise.

Ⓛ Listening Skills

The listening skills tasks are designed to help students develop strategies before listening, while listening, and after listening.

Ⓢ Speaking Skills

Students learn how to participate in formal and informal situations at universities, including sharing opinions, presenting research, and creating extended oral presentations. These skills and tasks were carefully selected to prepare students for university study.

Ⓥ Vocabulary Skills

Vocabulary learning is an essential part of academic preparation. Tasks throughout the books focus on particular sets of vocabulary that are important for reading in a particular subject area as well as vocabulary from the Academic Word List.

Ⓝ Note Taking Skills

In order to succeed in university courses, students need to be able to take notes effectively. Each unit teaches a range of note taking skills, ranging from organizational strategies and listening for key numbers to using your notes to prepare for tests.

Preparing for Authentic Listening

B Use information and ideas from the passage to answer these questions.

1. How are Mars and Earth similar? How are they different?
2. What makes life on Earth possible?

C Read these questions and then discuss your responses in a group.

1. Do you think life exists on Mars? In what form?
2. Do you also think life might exist outside our solar system? Explain your answer.

2 Listening to directions 🄛 🄢

Teachers usually give directions to their students orally. The ability to follow those directions is an important skill. But to follow directions, first you need to make sure you understand them! Practice these skills in the following activity.

A Look at the diagram below. It's called a Venn diagram. It shows similarities and differences.

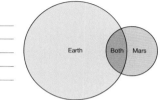

B Listen and follow the speaker's directions.

C Compare your diagram with a partner's. Discuss any differences in the way that you completed the diagram.

> Students develop a range of **skills** to help them **anticipate and prepare** for the listening tasks.

> The first listenings are **authentic interviews**, in which students develop **skills such as listening for main ideas and details.**

2 Listening for supporting details 🄝 🄛

Supporting details give more information about the main ideas of a lecture. They often consist of facts, definitions, examples, reasons, and explanations. In an outline, supporting details are indented and listed under the main ideas.

Earth is the third planet from the sun.

A Look at the outline for Part 1 of the lecture below. Then read the list of supporting details and think about where they might go in the outline.

Inside Planet Earth

I. Background information (main idea)

_____ (supporting detail)
_____ (supporting detail)
_____ (supporting detail)
_____ (supporting detail)
_____ (supporting detail)

Supporting Details

1. 5th largest planet in solar system
2. scientists use seismic waves (energy) to study Earth's layers
3. distance from N pole to S pole = about 13,000 kilometers
4. Earth's 3 main layers: crust, mantle, core
5. 3rd planet from sun

B Watch or listen to Part 1 of the lecture. As you listen, write the number of each supporting detail in the outline in Step A in the order that you hear it.

Academic Listening and Speaking

Sharing ideas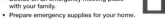

> Your understanding of a topic deepens when you share ideas with others.

A Read the volcano emergency plan. Look up any words you do not know in your dictionary.

Volcano Emergency Plan

Before an eruption
- Make an escape route from your house.
- Decide on an emergency meeting place with your family.
- Prepare emergency supplies for your home.

During an eruption
- Go to an emergency shelter. If there is no shelter in your neighborhood, try to move to high ground.
- Put a wet cloth over your mouth and nose to protect against smoke and ash in the air.

After an eruption
- Stay away from areas with lava, ash, or smoke.
- Protect your eyes, nose, mouth, and skin when you go outside.

B Work with a partner. Take turns giving each other advice about what you should do before, during, and after an eruption. Use some of these expressions for giving advice:

You should . . .   You ought to . . .   It's a good idea to . . .   You had better . . .

Example: *Before an eruption, you should make an escape route from your house.*

C Are there any other actions that can be added to the volcano emergency plan? Tell your partner your ideas.

> **Post-listening activities** help students **analyze and understand** the authentic inverviews.

---

3 In Your Own Voice

In this section, you are going to brainstorm the good points and bad points about each of the seasons. Then you will participate in a group debate in which you support your favorite season.

Thinking critically about the topic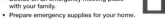

A Make a chart like the one below on a separate piece of paper. Working in a small group, discuss good points and bad points about each season. Write them in the chart.

	Good Points	Bad Points
Winter		
Spring		
Summer		
Fall		

B Choose the season you feel has the most good points, or the most important good points. Discuss why this season is "better" than the other seasons.

C Debate this issue with another small group that has chosen a different season. Take turns presenting the ideas in your chart and explaining why you chose the season you did. You can use some of the expressions below.

Presenting your ideas
There are many reasons we think . . . is the best season. First, . . .
Another reason we like . . . is that . . .
In addition, we think . . .

Responding to the other team
I'm afraid we don't agree with you, because . . .
I can see your point, but . . .
Yes, that may be true. However, . . .

> Students then study and practice using discrete **speaking skills**, as they express their own opinions about the **academic content**.

Academic Lectures and Note Taking

4 Academic Listening and Note Taking

In this section, you are going to hear and take notes on a two-part lecture by Anthony Modesto, MD. In his lecture, "Systems of the Human Body," Dr. Modesto will describe three systems of the human body: the digestive system, the respiratory system, and the cardiovascular system. The first part of his lecture focuses on the digestive system.

BEFORE THE LECTURE

1 Building background knowledge on the topic Ⓥ Ⓢ

A Work with a partner. Can you identify the organs of the human body in this illustration? Use the words in the box to label each organ. Look up any words you do not know in your dictionary.

esophagus	large intestine	mouth	small intestine	trachea
heart	lungs	nose	stomach	veins and arteries

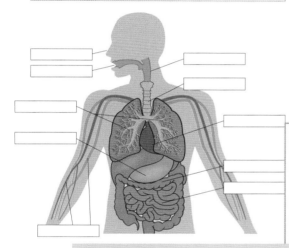

152 Unit 4 Life on Earth

> The full-color **design mirrors university textbooks**, providing students with an **authentic university experience**.

> Each unit provides extensive instruction and practice in **taking notes**, helping **students succeed** in university courses.

> Academic lectures take place in real college classrooms, complete with interactions between professors and students.

2 Taking notes in a flowchart Ⓝ Ⓛ

A flowchart clearly shows the steps in a process. Organizing your notes in a flowchart will help you understand and remember the process better.

A Look at the partial notes from Part 1 of Dr. Modesto's lecture. Think about what kind of information is missing from the flowchart.

<u>Digestive System</u>
- body uses energy in food
- proc of bkng down food, releasing nutr into body = digestion

> MOUTH—
> chew food—b/come
> soft, sm pieces

↓

> musc squeeze + mix w/
> chem. ➔ thick soup
> (can last hours)

↓

> SMALL INTESTINE–
> _____ pass through
> the _____
> into the _____

↓ leftover food

> _____ –
> Moves waste out of the
> _____

whole proc ∼ _____ hrs

◀ **B** Watch or listen to Part 1 of the lecture. Fill in the missing information in Step A.

📹 **C** Work with a partner and compare flowcharts.

Chapter 8 Humans **155**

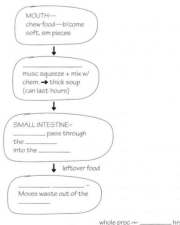

xiii

Academic Vocabulary and Oral Presentations

Unit 2 Academic Vocabulary Review

This section reviews the vocabulary from Chapters 3 and 4. Some of the words that you needed to learn to understand the content of this unit are specific to its topics. Other words are more general. They appear across different academic fields and are extremely useful for all students to know. For a complete list of all the Academic Word List words in this book, see the Appendix on page 180.

A Read the sentences and fill in the blanks with a form of the word.

1. **access (n), accessible (adj):**
   Having _____ to clean water is important for the health of any community.

2. **adapt (v), adaptation (n):**
   Many animals have been able to _____ to their surroundings.

3. **consequence (n), consequently (adv):**
   Without rain, rivers can dry up, and _____ animals sometimes have to go to other places to find water or food.

4. **constant (adj), constantly (adv):**
   Earth's water is _____ changing in form.

5. **cooperate (v), cooperation (n):**
   All countries should _____ to make sure we have clean water for everyone.

6. **environment (n), environmental (adj):**
   Bottled water is bad for the _____.

7. **location (n), located (adj):**
   A large amount of the world's freshwater is _____ in Canada.

8. **region (n), regional (adj):**
   The bottom of the ocean is the last unexplored _____ on Earth.

9. **transport (v), transportation (n):**
   Water is not only for drinking; it has also been used for _____ for centuries.

10. **resource (n), resourceful (adj):**
    We should all learn to look at water as a precious natural _____ that shouldn't be wasted.

Academic vocabulary development is **critical to student success**. Each unit includes **intensive vocabulary practice**, including words from the Academic Word List.

Oral Presentation

As a student, you will often participate in group presentations. Preparing and giving a group presentation helps you develop collaboration and leadership skills. Group presentations have to be carefully structured so that all members have an opportunity to speak. You should practice your presentation with your group members so that you can transition smoothly from one speaker to the next.

BEFORE THE PRESENTATION

1 Collect data

For this presentation, you will collect data about daily water usage. You will share the results with your group members. Then the group will make a usage report.

A Make a water usage journal like the one below. For one day, write down every activity you do that requires water. If possible, include the approximate amount of water you use.

	TASK	NOTES
Morning	flushed toilet brushed teeth washed face drank coffee (2 cups)	I usually leave the water on while I'm brushing my teeth. I could use less water if I turned off the tap.
Afternoon		
Evening		

B Share your water usage journal with your group members. Create a water usage report like the one below. Include every activity from each member's journal and the total number of times it occurred in one day.

Students create **oral presentations**, applying the vocabulary and academic content they study in each unit, and **preparing them to speak in a university classroom.**

To the student

Welcome to *Academic Encounters 1 Listening and Speaking: The Natural World!*

The *Academic Encounters* series gets its name because in this series you will *encounter*, or meet, the kinds of *academic* texts (lectures and readings), *academic* language (grammar and vocabulary), and *academic* tasks (taking tests, writing papers, and giving presentations) that you will encounter when you study an academic subject area in English. The goal of the series, therefore, is to prepare you for that encounter.

The approach of *Academic Encounters 1 Listening and Speaking: The Natural World*, may be different from what you are used to in your English studies. In this book, you are asked to study an academic subject area and be responsible for learning that information, in the same way as you might study in a college or university course. You will find that as you study this information, you will at the same time improve your English language proficiency and develop the skills that you will need to be successful when you come to study in your own academic subject area in English.

In *Academic Encounters 1 Listening and Speaking: The Natural World* for example, you will learn:

- what to listen for in academic lectures
- how to think critically about what you have heard
- how to participate in conversations and more formal discussions
- how to give oral presentations in an academic style
- methods of preparing for tests
- strategies for dealing with new vocabulary
- note-taking and study techniques

This course is designed to help you study in English in *any* subject matter. However, because during the study of this book, you will learn a lot of new information about research findings and theories in the field of sociology, you may feel that by the end you have enough background information to one day take and be successful in an introductory course in sociology in English.

We certainly hope that you find *Academic Encounters 1 Listening and Speaking: The Natural World* useful. We also hope that you will find it to be enjoyable. It is important to remember that the most successful learning takes place when you enjoy what you are studying and find it interesting.

Author's acknowledgments

I would very much like to thank Cambridge University Press for allowing me to remain involved with the Academic Encounters series and participate in the revision of the Listening-Speaking book. In particular I would like to thank series editor Bernard Seal, editorial manager Christopher Sol Cruz, development editor Michael Ryall, and contributing writer Mary Ann Maynard.

I would also like to thank fellow author Kim Sanabria for being a great source of ideas and feedback at the start of the project; my wonderful friend and colleague Jennifer Wharton for all her help (and shared venting!); and my husband for his consistent support and enthusiasm.

Finally, as with the first edition, this book would not be possible without the generous contributions of the original interviewees and lecturers, whose words and voices inspired every page.

Yoneko Kanaoka

Publisher's acknowledgments

The first edition of *Academic Encounters* has been used by many teachers in many institutions all around the world. Over the years, countless instructors have passed on feedback about the series, all of which has proven invaluable in helping to direct the vision for the second edition. More formally, a number of reviewers also provided us with a detailed analysis of the series, and we are especially grateful for their insights. We would therefore like to extend particular thanks to the following instructors:

Lynda Dalgish, Concordia College, Bronxville, New York
Nancy Hardee, Northwest Missouri State University, Maryville, Missouri
Ursala McCormick, Lewis & Clark College, Portland, Oregon
Roberta Steinberg, Mount Ida College, Newton, Massachusetts

Unit 1
Planet Earth

In this unit, you are going to learn about some of the natural features that make Earth unique. Chapter 1 looks at Earth's physical structure. You will hear an interview with a scientist and listen to people talking about interesting landmarks in different parts of the world. Then you will hear a lecture that gives you a look inside our planet, from its surface down to its center. Chapter 2 discusses some of the ways in which Earth's surface is always moving and changing. You will hear three people describe their firsthand experiences with Earth's movement. Then you will hear a lecture about three kinds of volcanoes and how they are formed.

Contents

In Unit 1, you will listen to and speak about the following topics.

Chapter 1 The Physical Earth	Chapter 2 The Dynamic Earth
Interview 1 A Geologist Talks	**Interview 1** Living Near an Active Volcano
Interview 2 Earth's Natural Beauty	**Interview 2** Living with Earthquakes
Lecture A Look Inside Planet Earth	**Lecture** Volcanoes

Skills

In Unit 1, you will practice the following skills.

Listening Skills	Speaking Skills
Listening to directions Listening for main ideas in an interview Listening for details Listening for main ideas in a lecture Listening for supporting details Listening for numerical information about distances and rates Understanding multiple-choice questions Drawing inferences	Sharing your knowledge Sharing your opinion Discussing what you have learned Interpreting a map Retelling what you have heard Sharing ideas Thinking critically about the topic Responding to a speaker
Vocabulary Skills	Note Taking Skills
Reading and thinking about the topic Understanding word parts Examining vocabulary in context Guessing vocabulary from context Building background knowledge on the topic Predicting the content	Organizing your notes in an outline Clarifying your notes with a partner Using your notes to label an illustration Focusing on the introduction Using telegraphic language Using your notes to make a study sheet

Learning Outcomes

Prepare and **deliver** an oral presentation about a natural disaster

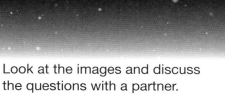

Chapter 1
The Physical Earth

Look at the images and discuss
the questions with a partner.

1. What do you know about our solar system?
2. What do you know about the planet Mars?

1 Getting Started

In this section, you are going to read about the similarities and differences between Earth
and Mars. You will fill out a graphic organizer that shows these similarities and differences.

1 Reading and thinking about the topic Ⓥ Ⓢ

> If you read or think about a topic before you hear it discussed, you will find the
> discussion much easier to understand.

A Read the following passage.

Earth and Mars are neighboring planets. Earth is the third planet from the sun, and Mars
is the fourth. In many ways, these two "neighbors" are very similar. In fact, Mars is more
like Earth than any other planet in our solar system. It has four seasons, just like Earth. Its
landforms also look very similar to those on Earth.

Both Mars and Earth have active volcanoes, although the volcanoes on Mars are much
larger. The biggest volcano on Mars, for example, is 600 kilometers wide. In comparison, the
largest volcano on Earth is about 120 kilometers in diameter.

Although they have many similarities, there are some important differences between these
two planets. One of the most important differences has to do with water. Some scientists think
there was once liquid water on Mars. That was probably millions of years ago, however. There
is no evidence that liquid water exists on Mars today.

Another important difference is in atmosphere – the gases and particles that surround
a planet. On Earth, the atmosphere is very thick. It contains heat and oxygen. The Martian
atmosphere is much thinner and weaker. It is so weak that most gas escapes into space.
With a weak atmosphere and no liquid water, Mars probably does not have any forms of life.

B Use information and ideas from the passage to answer these questions.

    1. How are Mars and Earth similar? How are they different?

    2. What makes life on Earth possible?

C Read these questions and then discuss your responses in a group.

    1. Do you think life exists on Mars? In what form?

    2. Do you also think life might exist outside our solar system? Explain your answer.

2 Listening to directions Ⓛ Ⓢ

Teachers usually give directions to their students orally. The ability to follow those directions is an important skill. But to follow directions, first you need to make sure you understand them! Practice these skills in the following activity.

A Look at the diagram below. It's called a Venn diagram. It shows similarities and differences.

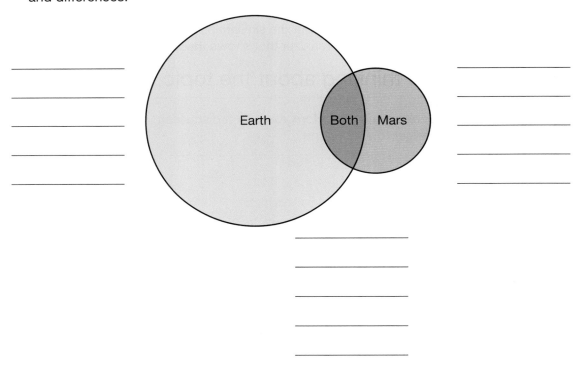

B Listen and follow the speaker's directions.

C Compare your diagram with a partner's. Discuss any differences in the way that you completed the diagram.

2 Real-Life Voices

In this section, you will hear Brad talk about his work as a geologist. Then you will hear Gaby and Jane describe some of the natural landmarks they have seen.

1 Understanding word parts Ⓥ Ⓢ

> When you see or hear new vocabulary, one way to guess the meaning is to look at each part of the word. Understanding word parts will help you increase your vocabulary quickly.

A Many English words come from the Greek language. This chart shows some common Greek roots and suffixes. What words do you know with these roots and suffixes?

Greek root	Meaning	Greek suffix	Meaning
bio-	life, living thing	-ist	a person who does something
geo-	earth, rocks	-graph	a writing tool or instrument
hydro-	water	-graphy	a systematic way of showing information using words or images
meteor-	sky, air, space	-(o)logy	the study of
seismo-	earthquake	-meter	a tool or device for measuring
volcano-	volcano		

B Combine roots and suffixes to make words that go with these definitions.

1. _____ = the study of Earth's structure
2. _____ = the study of life on Earth
3. _____ = a machine that measures the strength of earthquakes
4. _____ = the study of weather
5. _____ = a scientist who studies volcanoes
6. _____ = mapmaking and the study of Earth's physical features

C Practice saying these words with a partner. The stressed syllable is underlined.

meteor<u>o</u>logy   bi<u>o</u>logist   seis<u>mo</u>graphy

volc<u>a</u>nology   hy<u>dro</u>logist   ge<u>o</u>graphy

2 Sharing your knowledge Ⓢ

> Sharing your knowledge with your classmates makes you more aware of what you know about a topic. It also helps you learn new information.

A Work with a partner to complete the sentences. Use the map below to find any answers you do not know.

1. Earth has _____ continents and _____ oceans.
2. The largest continent is _____ and the smallest continent is _____ .
3. The highest mountain on Earth is _____ .
4. The lowest point on Earth is _____ .
5. The longest river is _____ .
6. The largest desert is _____ .

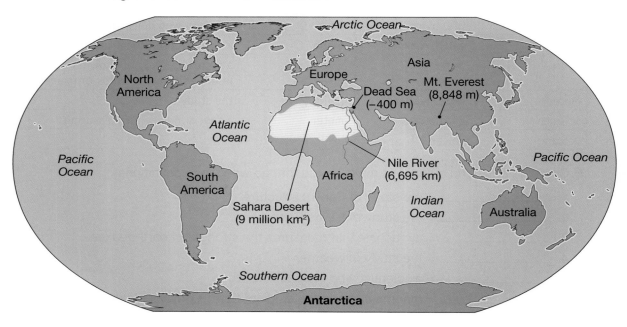

B Check your answers to Step A at the bottom of this page.

C Share your knowledge of Earth. Discuss the following questions with your partner.

1. How many continents have you been to? Name them.
2. How many oceans have you seen? Name them.
3. Have you ever climbed a mountain? Which one? How high was it?
4. Name one river and one lake you have been to.
5. Have you ever been to a desert? Talk about your experience.

1 Examining vocabulary in context **V**

Here are some words and phrases from the interview with Brad, printed in **bold** and given in the context in which you will hear them. They are followed by definitions.

It's . . . the study of the **composition** and dynamics of Earth: *the way something is made and the way its parts fit together*

. . . the composition and **dynamics** of Earth: *movement; change*

. . . from its center to its **surface**: *the top layer*

We . . . **measure** the size and shape of each beach: *to find the size, length, or amount*

. . . a **long-term** erosion problem: *continuing for a long period of time*

. . . the beaches are **eroding**: *disappearing or wearing away because of wind and water*

2 Listening for main ideas in an interview **L** **N**

Main ideas are the most important points that a speaker wants to make. In an interview, you can often understand the main ideas by paying close attention to the interviewer's questions.

A Read the topics below.

- The meaning of *geology* ☐
- The reason Brad became a geologist ☐
- The bad points about being a geologist ☐
- The project Brad is working on now ☐
- Brad's future goals ☐
- Brad's feelings about geology ☐

B Now listen to the interview with Brad. Listen for the interviewer's questions to help you understand the main ideas of the interview. Check (✓) each topic in Step A that you hear discussed.

C Summarize each main idea in the interview by completing the following sentences. Then compare your answers as a class.

Geologists study _____ .

When Brad was growing up, he asked many questions about _____ .

At his job right now, Brad is measuring _____ .

Brad thinks that geology is _____ .

1 Examining vocabulary in context

Here are some words and phrases from the interview printed in **bold** and given in the context in which you will hear them. They are followed by definitions.

The Grand Canyon is a very **popular** place: *liked by a lot of people*

And there are **cliffs** that are all different colors: *tall rocks with steep sides*

. . . it's **formed** out of rock: *made*

. . . one of the most visited **sites** in Australia: *a place where something is*

It's a **massive**, red rock: *very big*

It's made up of very, very hard **minerals**: *natural substances that are commonly found in the earth*

300 million years old? **Incredible**: *difficult to believe*

We have a lot of unique and **stunning** natural places: *beautiful, impressive*

If you look at it from far away, it looks **smooth**: *flat, with no bumps or rough parts*

2 Listening for details

Details explain, describe, or give more information about main ideas. Listening for details will help you improve your listening comprehension.

A The chart below shows the main ideas and some of the details Gaby and Jane will talk about in their interview. Notice that the notes are not complete sentences. Look at the photographs on the next page and think about other descriptive phrases that could go in the chart.

Main ideas	Details	
	Grand Canyon	**Uluru (Ayers Rock)**
What it looks like	*big – seems to go on forever* *cliffs – different colors*	
Its colors		*reddish-brown* *can change to pink, purple, gray depending on time of day*
The speakers' thoughts and feelings	*one of the most beautiful things ever seen* *lucky to see it*	
How it was formed		*layers of rock were lifted out of the earth* *softer rocks eroded – Uluru is what's left*

🔊 **B** Now listen to the interview with Gaby and Jane. Take notes as you listen. Add as many details as you can to the chart in Step A.

C Work with a partner. Take turns telling each other the similarities and differences between the Grand Canyon and Uluru. Here are some useful words for comparing:

Grand Canyon

Uluru, also known as Ayers Rock

Similarities	Differences
and, both, also, too, as well	*but, while, however*
Example: *The Grand Canyon **and** Uluru are **both** very beautiful.*	Example: *The Grand Canyon is in the United States, **but** Uluru is in Australia.*

Sharing your opinion Ⓢ

Sharing your opinion is a good way to review what you know and to deepen your understanding of a topic.

A A *landmark* is a well-known feature that is easy to recognize. Read the information about each natural landmark below. Which location looks most interesting to you?

B Work with a partner. Tell your partner about your choice. Use some of these expressions to share your opinion:

I think _____ looks most interesting because . . .

Another interesting place I know about is . . .

C Discuss the following questions as a class.

Which location in Step A is most attractive to you? Why?

Has anyone been to one of these famous natural landmarks? Tell the class about it.

MT. FUJI, JAPAN

- Japan's most famous landmark
- The country's highest mountain (3,776 meters)
- 200,000 people climb it every year
- Its beautiful shape is the subject of art, poems, and songs

NIAGARA FALLS
Canada / United States

- The world's most popular waterfalls
- Located on the border between Canada and the United States
- 51 meters high, more than 1,000 meters wide
- 91 million liters of water flow over the falls every minute
- A beautiful and powerful natural wonder

GUILIN MOUNTAINS
CHINA

- Magical, mysterious, limestone mountains
- Unique and strange shapes sometimes look like animals or people
- Beautiful, misty landscape appears in many Chinese poems and paintings

3 In Your Own Voice

In this section, you will prepare some information about a natural landmark in your country. Then you will tell your classmates about the landmark.

Discussing what you have learned Ⓢ

> Finding ways to discuss what you have learned is a good way to deepen your understanding of new subject matter.

A Make a list of famous natural landmarks in your country. Write down the names of well-known mountains, valleys, bodies of water, rock formations, and any other natural landmarks you can think of.

B Choose one natural landmark in Step A. Complete the worksheet below. Use the Internet to find any information you do not know.

Name of landmark: _____

PICTURE
(Draw or attach a picture of your landmark here.)

Location _____   How it was formed _____

Age _____   _____

Size   Famous or unique points _____

Height _____   _____

Length _____   _____

Depth _____   _____

Width _____   _____

C Tell your classmates about your landmark. Use some of the sentences below to explain your information.

I'd like to tell you about _____ , a famous natural landmark in

_____ .

_____ is very big. It is _____ kilometers high/deep/wide/long.

_____ is very old. It was formed _____ years ago by . . .

_____ is famous for several reasons. First, . . . /Second, . . . /Finally, . . .

Do you have any questions about _____ ?

4 Academic Listening and Note Taking

In this section, you will hear and take notes on a lecture by Dr. Laura Barbieri, a scientist who studies planets. In her lecture, "A Look Inside Planet Earth," Dr. Barbieri will first give some general information about our planet. Then she will describe Earth's layers in detail.

BEFORE THE LECTURE

1 Listening for main ideas in a lecture Ⓛ Ⓝ

> When you listen to a lecture, the most important step is to identify the main ideas. Good lecturers will use phrases like these to help you notice the main ideas:
>
> *There are several important points I'll talk about today . . .*
> *The first point is . . .*
> *Now let's move on to . . .*
> *Next I would like to discuss . . .*
> *Finally, . . .*

A The sentences below are from the lecture. One sentence introduces the topic. Mark that sentence with a T. The other sentences are main ideas. Decide the order in which you think they will appear. Write 1 next to the main idea that you think will come first in the lecture, 2 next to the second main idea, and so on.

_____ Now, I'd like to discuss each of the three main layers of Earth. First, the crust. . . . There are two kinds of crust: oceanic and continental.

_____ But first, I want to give you some background information about our planet.

_____ Finally, continuing down toward the center of the planet, we come to the core. The core can be divided into two parts: an outer core and an inner core.

_____ Today, let's look inside planet Earth and discuss its internal structure.

_____ Moving down from the crust, the next layer of Earth is called the mantle.

B Work with a partner and compare answers to Step A.

C Watch or listen and check your answers. You will hear the main ideas in the order in which they appear in the lecture.

2 Organizing your notes in an outline Ⓝ

Using an outline can be an effective way to organize notes. In an outline, numbers and letters show relationships between main ideas and details. Topics that explain main ideas in more detail are called subtopics and are listed underneath the main ideas.

A Look at the outline for the lecture below. Turn back to "Listening for main ideas in a lecture" on page 11. Fill in the blanks below with the main ideas of the lecture. You do not have to write whole sentences, only topics and ideas.

<u>Inside Planet Earth</u>

(lecture topic)

I.   Background information (main idea)

II. Crust (main idea)

    A. _____ (subtopic)

    B. _____ (subtopic)

III. _____ = next layer down from crust (main idea)

IV. _____ = center of planet (main idea)

    A. _____ (subtopic)

    B. _____ (subtopic)

B With a partner, answer the following questions: How many main ideas are there in the lecture? How many main ideas have subtopics?

1 Guessing vocabulary from context ⓥ

When you hear or read words that you do not know, pay attention to the words in the surrounding context. The context can give you clues that will help you understand the new words. Using your knowledge of related words will also help you.

A The following items contain important vocabulary from Part 1 of the lecture. Work with a partner. Using the context and your knowledge of related words, take turns guessing the meanings of the words in **bold**.

_____ **1.** . . . oceans, rivers and lakes, **soil** and rocks.

_____ **2.** Let's look inside planet Earth and discuss its **internal** structure.

_____ **3.** Let's look inside planet Earth and discuss its internal **structure**.

_____ **4.** If we draw a line directly through the center of the planet, the distance from the **North Pole** to the **South Pole** is almost 13,000 kilometers.

_____ **5.** Earth is made up of three main **layers**.

_____ **6.** The crust is the **outer** layer of Earth.

_____ **7.** Scientists can study these three layers by using **seismic** waves.

B Work with your partner. Match the bold terms in the sentences in Step A with their definitions below. Check your answers in a dictionary if necessary.

a. the center points at the top and bottom of Earth

b. the different parts that together make up one thing

c. energy that moves through Earth like water moves in the ocean

d. something that covers a surface or area

e. the material on the ground in which plants grow; earth

f. on the outside of something

g. on the inside of something

2 Listening for supporting details N L

Supporting details give more information about the main ideas of a lecture.
They often consist of facts, definitions, examples, reasons, and explanations.
In an outline, supporting details are indented and listed under the main ideas.

Earth is the third
planet from the sun.

A Look at the outline for Part 1 of the lecture below. Then read the list of supporting
details and think about where they might go in the outline.

Inside Planet Earth

I. Background information (main idea)

_____ (supporting detail)

_____ (supporting detail)

_____ (supporting detail)

_____ (supporting detail)

_____ (supporting detail)

Supporting Details

1. 5th largest planet in solar system
2. scientists use seismic waves (energy) to study Earth's layers
3. distance from N pole to S pole = about 13,000 kilometers
4. Earth's 3 main layers: crust, mantle, core
5. 3rd planet from sun

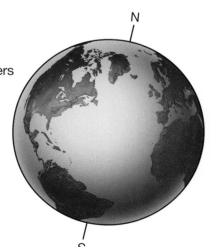

B Watch or listen to Part 1 of the lecture. As you listen,
write the number of each supporting detail in the
outline in Step A in the order that you hear it.

1 Guessing vocabulary from context Ⓥ

> Illustrations can provide helpful context when you hear or read new words. Use the information in the illustrations to guess the meaning of words you do not know. Illustrations can also deepen your understanding of the words you already know.

A The pictures below illustrate some ideas from Dr. Barbieri's lecture. Study the pictures and notice the key vocabulary words in bold.

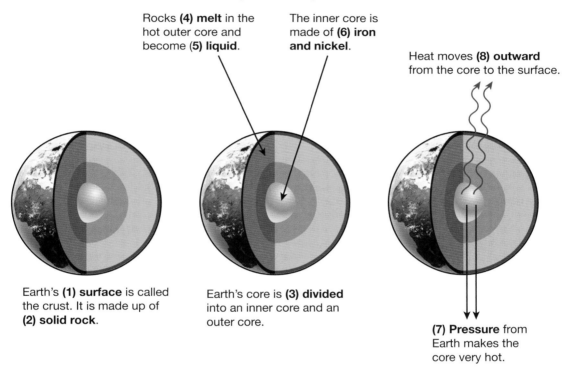

Rocks **(4) melt** in the hot outer core and become **(5) liquid**.

The inner core is made of **(6) iron and nickel**.

Heat moves **(8) outward** from the core to the surface.

Earth's **(1) surface** is called the crust. It is made up of **(2) solid rock**.

Earth's core is **(3) divided** into an inner core and an outer core.

(7) Pressure from Earth makes the core very hot.

B Work with a partner. Match the vocabulary words with their definitions. Write the number from Step A on the line next to the correct definition.

_____ **a.** hard, heavy metals that are common on Earth

_____ **b.** the force or weight of one thing on another thing

_____ **c.** firm; hard

_____ **d.** the opposite of the word that matches definition "c"

_____ **e.** away from something

_____ **f.** the upper layer of an area of land

_____ **g.** change from a solid into a liquid

_____ **h.** separated into two or more parts

2 Listening for supporting details ⓝ ⓛ

A Look at the outline for Part 2 of the lecture below. Then read the list of supporting details and think about where they might go in the outline.

<u>Inside Planet Earth</u>

II. Crust (main idea)

_____ (supporting detail)

   A. Oceanic (subtopic)

_____ (supporting detail)
_____ (supporting detail)

   B. Continental (subtopic)

_____ (supporting detail)
_____ (supporting detail)

III. Mantle = next layer down from crust (main idea)

_____ (supporting detail)
_____ (supporting detail)
_____ (supporting detail)

IV. Core = center of planet (main idea)
   A. Outer core (subtopic)

_____ (supporting detail)

   B. Inner core (subtopic)

_____ (supporting detail)
_____ (supporting detail)
_____ (supporting detail)

Supporting details

1. temperature as high as 4,000°C
2. land areas
3. high pressure, high temperature
4. lower – hot and soft
5. covered by oceans
6. much thicker than crust (2,900 km)

7. made of solid rock
8. very hot – liquid rock
9. 6–11 km thick
10. 30–40 km thick
11. iron and nickel
12. upper – cool, solid rock

B Watch or listen to Part 2 of the lecture. As you listen, write the number of each supporting detail in the outline in Step A under the correct main idea or subtopic.

3 Clarifying your notes with a partner Ⓝ Ⓢ

A good way to check your notes after a lecture is to review them with a classmate. Explaining your notes helps you review information and understand it better. When you ask your classmate questions about the lecture, you can fill in any information you missed.

A Work with a partner. Review your notes from Parts 1 and 2 of the lecture. Take turns explaining each section of the outline, and help each other correct or add information. Use some of the following expressions as you review:

I heard . . . Is that what you heard, too?

I think the lecturer said . . .

My information is different. I wrote . . .

I didn't understand the part about . . .

B As a class, discuss parts of the lecture that you still do not understand.

AFTER THE LECTURE

Using your notes to label an illustration Ⓝ Ⓢ

A good way to apply the information you have learned in a lecture is to make and label an illustration. In this way, you show how well you understood the lecture content.

A Using your notes from Dr. Barbieri's lecture, label each part of the illustration below.

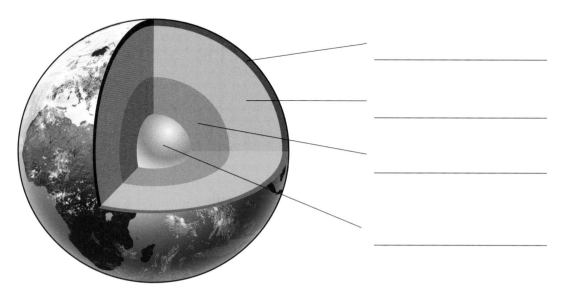

_____

_____

_____

_____

B Work with a partner and compare your illustrations.

Chapter 2
The Dynamic Earth

Look at the picture above and answer the questions with a partner.

1. What is happening in the picture?
2. Are there any volcanoes in your country? If yes, are they active (moving) or dormant (not moving)?
3. How are volcanoes formed?

1 Getting Started

In this section, you will learn more about Earth's crust and how it is always moving. You will also listen to a recording about the movement of oceans, mountains, and islands.

1 Reading and thinking about the topic

A Read the following passage.

As you learned in Chapter 1, Earth has three main layers: the core, the mantle, and the crust. The thin crust is made up of hard rock, but it is not one solid piece of rock. Instead, it is broken into many pieces, called *plates*. These plates lie on top of the hotter and softer mantle. There are about 12 very large plates and several smaller plates (see the map on page 20). These plates are moving slowly over the surface of our planet. This movement is called *plate tectonics*.

Earth's plates move in different directions. Sometimes they move away from each other, and sometimes they crash into each other. In other cases, two plates may rub against each other, side by side. These movements can cause volcanoes or earthquakes. They can also form mountains and valleys. Although Earth may seem to be very stable, it is actually changing all the time.

B Answer the following questions according to the information in the passage.

   1. Describe Earth's crust.

   2. Describe three ways that Earth's plates can move.

   3. What are some effects of plate tectonics on Earth's surface?

C Read the following questions and share your answers with a partner.

   1. Are there many earthquakes where you live? Where and how often do they happen?

   2. Have you ever seen a volcano? If so, describe what you saw.

   3. Name one earthquake and one volcanic eruption that you have heard about.

2 Listening for numerical information about distances and rates Ⓛ Ⓢ

> Listening for numerical information (numbers) can be difficult in a second language. Here is some information to help you understand numbers related to distances and rates.

1 centimeter (cm) = 10 millimeters (mm)	per year = every year
1 meter (m) = 100 cm	rate = speed; number of times that something happens
1 kilometer (km) = 1,000 m	
NOTE: Say *point* for a decimal point in a number. For example: You read: Earth is 4.6 billion years old. You say: *Earth is four point six billion years old.*	

A Before you listen to information about the movement of Earth, read the following sentences. Try to predict if you will hear millimeters, centimeters, or kilometers.

   1. The Atlantic Ocean is growing at a rate of about _____ per year.

   2. The Himalaya Mountains are rising at a rate of about _____ per year.

   3. Two plates in California are moving side by side in opposite directions at a rate of almost _____ per year.

   4. The Hawaiian Islands are moving northwest toward Japan at a rate of about _____ per year.

🔊 **B** Listen and fill in the numbers in Step A. Compare answers with a partner.

C Working with your partner and using the information in Step A, answer the questions about distances and rates.

1. At its widest point, the Atlantic Ocean is 4,830 kilometers wide. How many years will it take to increase to 4,831 kilometers?

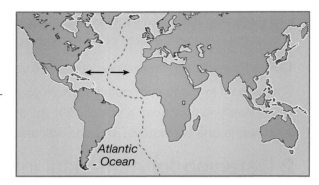

_____

2. Mt. Everest, in the Himalayas, is the highest mountain in the world. Its height is currently 8,848 meters. How tall will Mt. Everest be in 400 years?

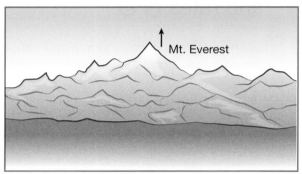

_____

3. The cities of San Francisco and Los Angeles, in California, are about 560 kilometers apart. A million years from now, will they be closer to each other or farther apart?

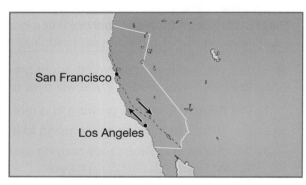

_____

4. The islands of Hawaii and Japan are about 6,200 kilometers apart. About how many years will it take for them to be 1 kilometer closer to each other?

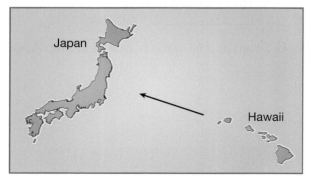

_____

D Check your answers to Step C at the bottom of page 21.

2 Real-Life Voices

In this section, you will hear an interview with Loren, who lives in Hawaii near an active volcano. Then Zack and Yoshiko will talk about earthquakes in California and Japan.

BEFORE THE INTERVIEWS

Interpreting a map ⓢ

> A map can present a great deal of information efficiently. It is important to be able to read and understand a map correctly.

Look at the map below. It shows the major plates of Earth's crust. It also shows the location of some of Earth's active volcanoes and recent earthquakes. After studying the map, look at the questions that follow it and discuss them with a partner.

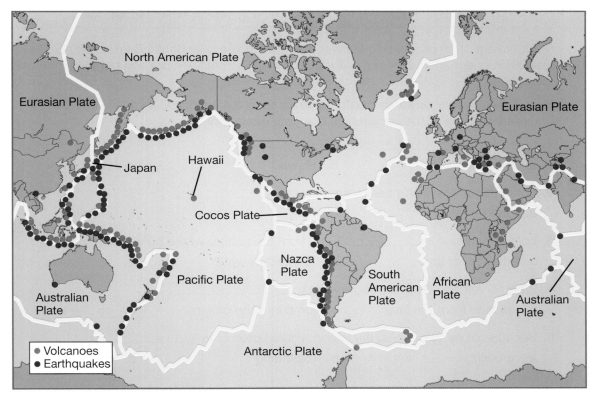

1. Find your country on the map. Is there a lot of activity from volcanoes or earthquakes there?
2. Which continent has had no active volcanoes and few earthquakes in recent years?
3. Where have most of Earth's volcanoes and earthquakes been located? Why?

Answers to "Listening for numerical information about distances and rates," Step C, page 20: 1. 40,000 years; 2. 8,850 meters; 3. farther apart; 4. about 14,286 years

Here are some words and expressions from the interview with Loren, printed in bold and given in the context in which you will hear them. They are followed by definitions.

... one of the most **dynamic** places on Earth: *always moving and changing*

... it has been **erupting** continuously since 1983: *sending smoke, ash, rock, and lava into the sky*

I will never forget ... seeing a huge **fountain of lava**: *hot, melted rock moving quickly up into the air*

It was just **spectacular** / It was **awesome**: *wonderful; impressive*

When the hot lava meets the ocean it creates a large cloud of **steam**: *gas that water becomes when it is very, very hot*

... the volcanoes in Hawaii usually do not **explode** strongly or suddenly: *to suddenly break apart, often with a loud noise and pieces that fly outward*

1 Understanding multiple-choice questions

> Students are often required to answer multiple-choice questions on tests. Be sure to read each question and all of the answer choices carefully before you begin.

A Read the following sentences before you listen to the interview. If you do not understand some of the vocabulary, use your dictionary.

1. Loren lives in _____ .
  a. Kilauea   **b.** Hawaii   **c.** Loihi

2. Loren thinks that living near a volcano is _____ .
  a. dangerous   **b.** tiring   **c.** exciting

3. Loren once saw a _____ from the school where he was working.
  a. fountain of lava   **b.** fountain of water   **c.** plane taking off

4. When a volcano erupts, people want to _____ .
  a. escape from the lava   **b.** jump into the ocean   **c.** go see the lava

5. Because of its volcanoes, the island where Loren lives is _____ .
  a. growing   **b.** exploding   **c.** sinking

B Now listen to the interview with Loren. As you listen, circle the correct answer to each question in Step A.

C Compare your answers with a partner. Then discuss the following questions:

1. Did you hear any surprising information in the interview? Explain.
2. Would you want to live near an active volcano? Why or why not?

2 Responding to a speaker ⓢ

> One way to show that you are listening during a conversation is to respond to the speaker with words or short phrases. These phrases (called rejoinders) show that you understand what is being said and that you are interested in the conversation.
> Here are some examples of common rejoinders:
>
> | | | |
> |---|---|---|
> | *That's really interesting.* | *Wow!* | *You're kidding!* |
> | *That sounds wonderful.* | *Awesome!* | *No way!* |
> | *That's great!* | *Really?* | *I can't believe it!* |

A Look at this excerpt from the interview with Loren. How does the interviewer show she is interested in the conversation?

Loren: . . . we have the world's most active volcano.

Interviewer: That sounds interesting! Can you tell me more about your volcano?

B Read the statements in the left column. Then match each one with the best response in the right column. The first one is done for you.

1. Kilauea is the world's most active volcano.
2. I want to try skydiving this weekend.
3. Last night my TV kept turning on by itself.
4. Tomorrow I leave on my trip to Europe.
5. Yesterday's sunset was red, yellow, and pink.
6. I can do 100 push-ups.

a. That's exciting!
b. Wow, that's incredible!
c. Really? That sounds dangerous.
d. That sounds beautiful.
e. Wow, that's interesting!
f. That's so weird!

C Work with a partner and compare your answers to Step B. Then take turns practicing the expressions. One partner should read a statement from the left column and the other partner should respond with the matching phrase.

D Now make your own statement. Your partner should respond appropriately.

Your statement: _____

Your partner's response: _____

Here are some words and expressions from the interview with Zack and Yoshiko, printed in bold and given in the context in which you will hear them. They are followed by definitions.

Many earthquakes happen when I'm asleep and I don't even **notice**: *be aware of something by seeing, hearing, or feeling it*

It just feels like a little **shaking**: *moving quickly up and down or side to side*

It felt like the floor became **liquid**: *not hard; like water*

. . . the **corners** of the office were going up and down: *the point where two walls of a room meet*

. . . have you had **similar** experiences in Japan?: *almost the same*

it's **no big deal**: *not serious or important*

. . . we had earthquake **drills**: *exercises in which people practice what to do in a dangerous situation*

. . . you make an **emergency** plan: *a plan for what to do in a dangerous situation or disaster*

1 Drawing inferences Ⓛ Ⓢ

Drawing inferences means understanding things that speakers do not say directly. You can draw inferences by using your background knowledge, context clues, and other information given by the speaker.

A Read the statements below. Zack and Yoshiko do not say these things directly, but you can infer whether they are true or false based on what you hear in the interview.

_____ **1.** Zack and Yoshiko have both experienced many earthquakes in their lives.

_____ **2.** Zack and Yoshiko usually feel afraid when an earthquake is happening.

_____ **3.** Zack had some emergency earthquake training at work.

_____ **4.** Zack and Yoshiko are well prepared for an earthquake.

_____ **5.** Zack and Yoshiko want to move away from San Francisco.

B Listen to the interview. Draw inferences based on what you hear and write *T* (True) or *F* (False) next to each statement in Step A. If you do not have enough information to draw an inference, write NS (Not sure) in the blank.

2 Retelling what you have heard ⓢ

One way to make sure you have understood what you have heard is to retell the information to the speaker or to another listener. You do not need to use the same words that the speaker used.

A Answer the following questions about Zack and Yoshiko. If necessary, listen to the interview one more time.

1. Where did Zack grow up? Where does he live now?
2. What does Zack think about small earthquakes?
3. What happened when Zack experienced a big earthquake?
4. Where did Yoshiko grow up? Where does she live now?
5. What does Yoshiko do when an earthquake happens?
6. How do Zack and Yoshiko prepare for earthquakes?

B With a partner, take turns retelling what you heard in the interview. Include the answers to the questions in Step A. Use the words in the vocabulary presentation on page 24 to help you retell the story.

Sharing ideas ⓢ

> Your understanding of a topic deepens when you share ideas with others.

A Read the volcano emergency plan. Look up any words you do not know in your dictionary.

Volcano Emergency Plan

Before an eruption
- Make an escape route from your house.
- Decide on an emergency meeting place with your family.
- Prepare emergency supplies for your home.

During an eruption
- Go to an emergency shelter. If there is no shelter in your neighborhood, try to move to high ground.
- Put a wet cloth over your mouth and nose to protect against smoke and ash in the air.

After an eruption
- Stay away from areas with lava, ash, or smoke.
- Protect your eyes, nose, mouth, and skin when you go outside.

B Work with a partner. Take turns giving each other advice about what you should do before, during, and after an eruption. Use some of these expressions for giving advice:

You should . . .   *You ought to . . .*   *It's a good idea to . . .*   *You had better . . .*

Example: *Before an eruption, you should make an escape route from your house.*

C Are there any other actions that can be added to the volcano emergency plan? Tell your partner your ideas.

3 In Your Own Voice

In this section, you will learn more about the movement of Earth's plates. You will gather evidence to support the theory of plate tectonics through reading, a hands-on task, interviews, and group and class discussions.

1 Sharing ideas ⑤

A Read the following passage about plate tectonics. Then discuss the question that follows with a partner.

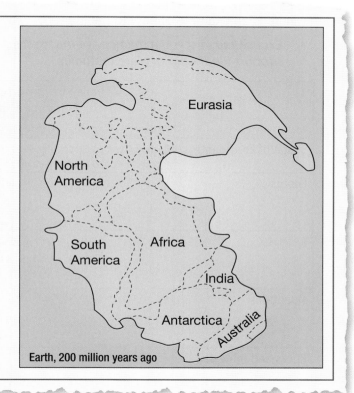

According to the theory of plate tectonics, the plates that make up Earth's crust are always moving. Scientists believe that 200 million years ago, all of Earth's plates were together in one large piece of land called Pangea. In other words, our planet had only one large continent and one large ocean! Over time, the plates slowly moved away from each other to form the continents and oceans we know today.

Earth, 200 million years ago

What kinds of evidence support the theory that all of Earth's continents were once connected?

B Turn to page 164. Trace the world map onto a piece of white paper. Use scissors to cut out the continents from your piece of paper. Try to fit the separate pieces together. Then discuss the following questions with your partner.

1. What do you notice about the shape of Earth's continents?
2. Is it easy or difficult to fit the continents together?
3. Does the shape of Earth's continents support the theory of plate tectonics?

C Work in a small group. Choose one of the following topics for your group: the shape of continents, fossils, animals, mountains, or rocks and minerals. Each topic provides evidence that supports the theory of plate tectonics.

D Turn to page 165 and find the evidence for your group's topic. Read the information and discuss it with your group members. Use the vocabulary list below to help you understand new words. When you are ready, turn back to this page. Do not look at the evidence for the next part of the activity!

Fossil: a very old animal or plant, or its shape, that you find in a rock

Suggest: show that something is probably true

Marsupials: animals that carry their babies in a pocket of skin on the mother's body

Mountain range: a group of mountains, usually in a line

E Interview members of the other groups and take notes in the chart below.
Here is an example of how to get started:

Excuse me, are you a member of the fossils group? Please tell me how fossils support the theory of plate tectonics.

Theory of plate tectonics Evidence chart	
Group	Notes
Shape of continents	When we look at the shape of today's continents, we can see that they can fit together like puzzle pieces.
Fossils	
Animals	
Mountains	
Rocks and minerals	

F Return to your group and review the five kinds of evidence in your chart. Then choose one person to present your group's evidence to the class. Here is an example:

My group is the shape of continents group. Today's continents can fit together like puzzle pieces. This is evidence that the continents were all together at one time in the past.

G After each group has presented its evidence, discuss the following questions as a class.

1. In your opinion, what is the strongest evidence supporting the theory of plate tectonics?

2. In the future, how could the shape and location of the continents and oceans change?

4 Academic Listening and Note Taking

In this section, you will hear and take notes on a two-part lecture given by Dr. Patricia Fryer, a volcanologist (a person who studies volcanoes). In her lecture "Volcanoes," Dr. Fryer will describe the basic structure of a volcano and then introduce three different types of volcanoes.

BEFORE THE LECTURE

1 Building background knowledge on the topic

> Learning background information and vocabulary before a lecture can help you understand the content better when you hear it.

A Review the scientific terms and definitions related to volcanoes. If there are any words you still don't understand, discuss them with a classmate.

crust: *the top layer of Earth*

mantle: *the layer below the crust*

magma: *melted rock that forms in Earth's mantle*

vent: *a hole in Earth's crust; magma moves through the vent to Earth's surface*

crater: *the bowl-shaped opening at the top of a volcano*

lava: *melted rock (magma) on the surface of Earth*

B Using the terms and definitions in Step A, label each part of the diagram below.

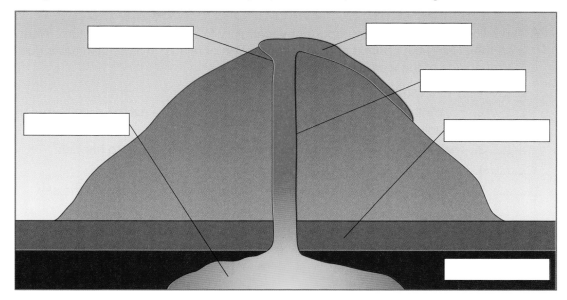

C The diagram in Step B is based on Dr. Fryer's lecture on volcanoes. Work with a partner. Compare your diagrams and then predict what you will hear in the lecture.

2 Focusing on the introduction N L

> Be sure to listen carefully and take notes during the introduction of a lecture. A good lecturer will state the main topic of the lecture and outline the major subtopics in the introduction. You may hear some of the following expressions.
>
> *Today I'd like to talk to you about . . .*   *Then I will describe . . .*
>
> *The topic of our lecture today is . . .*   *After that, we'll move on to . . .*
>
> *I'd like to start by explaining . . .*   *Finally, we'll discuss . . .*

A Watch or listen to the introduction of Dr. Fryer's lecture. As you listen, circle the phrases she uses to explain her plan for the lecture.

1. (*Today's lecture is going to be about / The topic of our lecture today is*) volcanoes.

2. (*In the first part of today's lecture, I will introduce / I'd like to start today's lecture by introducing*) the basic structure of a volcano . . .

3. (*After that, we'll move on to / Then I'll describe*) three basic types of volcanoes: shield volcanoes, composite volcanoes, and super volcanoes.

4. (*Finally, we'll discuss / In the final part of the lecture, I'll discuss*) some of the signs that volcanoes exhibit right before they are going to erupt.

B Compare your answers with a partner.

LECTURE PART 1   The Basic Structure of a Volcano

1 Guessing vocabulary from context V

A The following items contain important vocabulary from Part 1 of the lecture. Work with a partner. Using the context and your knowledge of related words, take turns guessing the meanings of the words in **bold**.

_____ **1.** . . . volcanoes are a really important **topic** . . .

_____ **2.** . . . we'll discuss some of the **signs** that volcanoes exhibit right before they are going to erupt.

_____ **3.** These are signs . . . that **warn** that an eruption is about to happen.

_____ **4.** . . . magma **flows** through the mantle . . .

_____ **5.** . . . clouds of **ash** and rock that rise thousands of meters into the sky.

B Work with your partner. Match the bold terms in the phrases in Step A with their definitions below. If necessary, use a dictionary to check your answers.

a. to tell someone about possible danger or trouble

b. soft, gray powder that is left after something burns

c. a subject that people talk or write about

d. signals or events that show what might happen in the future

e. moves easily, without stopping

2 Using telegraphic language Ⓝ Ⓛ

When you listen to a lecture, it is not possible to write down everything the lecturer says. Good note takers are able to write down the most important information in as few words as possible. *Telegraphic language* will help you do this quickly. Telegraphic language includes key words that carry information, but usually does not include:

Articles (*a*, *an*, and *the*)

The verb *to be* and other linking verbs

Prepositions and pronouns

Examples

You hear: Volcanoes make about 75 percent of all the rocks on the surface of Earth.
You write: *Volcanoes make 75% rocks on Earth*

You hear: Volcanoes are a really important topic when we talk about our natural world.
You write: *Volcanoes – important topic – natural world*

A Look at some sample sentences from Dr. Fryer's lecture. Underline the key words. Cross out any unnecessary words.

1. Magma comes from ~~Earth's~~ mantle, ~~which is a layer~~ deep below ~~Earth's~~ surface.

2. The upper mantle is from 80 to 150 kilometers below Earth's surface, and the temperatures here are so high that rocks start to melt and become magma.

3. Usually an eruption starts because an earthquake breaks the rock at the top of the mantle and creates an opening.

4. The magma then rises through the opening in the solid rock and moves toward the surface of Earth.

5. Finally, the magma comes out of an opening in the crust, called a vent.

B Look at the notes from Part 1 of Dr. Fryer's lecture. With a partner, try to figure out what the telegraphic language means.

Part 1: The Basic Structure of a Volcano

_____ Magma flows through mantle, pushes against rock

_____ Magma on top of Earth's surface = lava

__1__ Volcanoes formed by hot, melted rock (magma) from mantle

_____ Volcano can be gentle (lava flows on surface) or powerful (clouds of ash, rock)

_____ Earthquake breaks rock – magma comes out opening in crust (vent)

_____ Upper mantle 80–150 km below surface; high temperatures melt rock

🔊 **C** Now watch or listen to Part 1 of the lecture. Number the notes in Step B in the order
📹 that you hear them discussed in the lecture.

LECTURE PART 2 Types of Volcanoes

1 Guessing vocabulary from context Ⓥ

A The sentences below contain important vocabulary from Part 2 of the lecture.
Work with a partner. Using the context and your knowledge of related words,
take turns trying to guess the meanings of the words in **bold**.

_____ **1.** I have math class on Mondays and Wednesdays and English class on
Tuesdays and Thursdays. In other words, I have an **alternating** schedule of
math and English.

_____ **2.** His new couch was too **broad** to fit through the narrow door. He will have to
find a smaller couch.

_____ **3.** Most people think volcanoes are shaped like a **cone**, even though they can
have other shapes as well.

_____ **4.** Although there are some small **cracks** in this mirror, I can still use it. I don't
want to buy a new mirror unless it breaks into pieces.

_____ **5.** After the heavy rain, many **craters** formed in the road. One hole was so big
that a car got stuck in it!

_____ **6.** The big earthquake caused a lot of **destruction**, including many homes
damaged, and many people were injured or even killed.

_____ **7.** It's easier to play golf on a flat course. If the ground is **sloping**, it's difficult to
hit the ball straight.

_____ **8.** Nowadays, the use of smart phones is **widespread**. It seems like people of
all ages have smart phones.

B Work with your partner. Match the bold terms in the sentences in Step A with their definitions below. If necessary, use a dictionary to check your answers.

- **a.** large from one side to the other; wide
- **b.** not flat; higher at one end than at the other
- **c.** great damage or harm
- **d.** a large, round hole that is shaped like a bowl
- **e.** happening in many places and to many people
- **f.** repeating one after the other in a regular pattern
- **g.** thin lines in something that is broken, but not separated into pieces
- **h.** a shape that is circular on one end and pointed on the other

2 Predicting the content

> Thinking about the topic and predicting what you are going to hear will help your listening comprehension. Use your background knowledge and key vocabulary to try to predict the content.

A Study the vocabulary chart below.

shield	*a large, broad piece of metal carried by people to protect themselves when fighting*
composite	*made of different parts or materials*
super	*more, bigger, or more powerful than others of the same kind*

Concrete is a composite material. It is made up of sand, gravel, and other materials that are mixed with water.

B In Dr. Fryer's lecture, you will hear about three types of volcanoes: shield volcanoes, composite volcanoes, and super volcanoes. Can you predict what each type of volcano looks like? Use the information in Step A and label the pictures of the volcanoes on page 36.

C Compare your answers with a partner. Explain how you predicted each type of volcano.

3 Using telegraphic language Ⓝ Ⓛ

A Look at the outline for Part 2 of Dr. Fryer's lecture. Think about the kind of information you need to complete the outline.

Part 2: Types of Volcanoes

I. Shield volcanoes

    A. Very big

    B. Lava flows from vent – gentle _____

    C. _____ cools, becomes hard

        Shape like shield: _____ , sloping sides

    D. Example: Mauna Loa, Hawaii

        Largest volcano – starts on _____ ,

        rises to _____

II. Composite volcanoes

    A. Smaller – 2,500 m

    B. Both explosive and gentle eruptions

        1. Explosive: layers of _____ pile up near

            _____

        2. Gentle: Lava flow covers ash, makes _____

        3. Composite = made up of _____

    C. Examples

        1. Mt. _____

        2. Mt. St. Helens (U.S.)

III. Super volcanoes

    A. Biggest volcanoes, most _____ eruptions

    B. Don't form _____ – leave huge _____

    C. Don't happen often but can cause _____

    D. Example: Toba

        1. _____ years ago in Indonesia

        2. Killed _____ on Earth

IV. Warning signs before an eruption

    A. _____

    B. Ground cracks

    C. Drinking water _____

    D. _____ starts to melt

B Now watch or listen to Part 2 of the lecture. Fill in the missing information in the outline using your own telegraphic language.

C Work with a partner and review your notes. Take turns explaining each section of the outline. Ask your partner about any information from the lecture that you did not understand.

Using your notes to make a study sheet 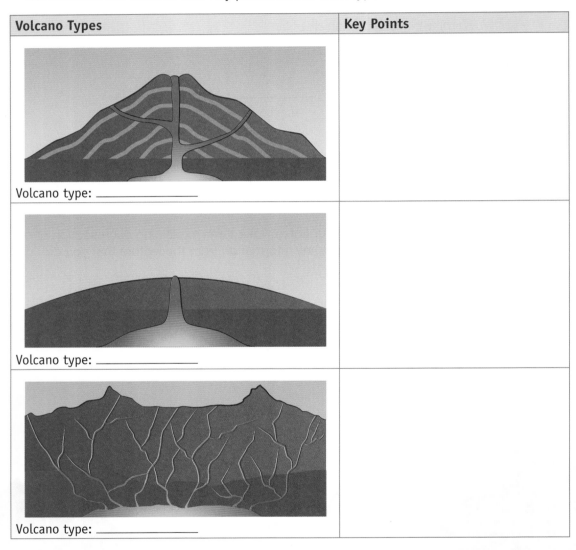 N S

A good way to prepare for a test is to make a study sheet. A study sheet will help you review the most important points.

A The study sheet below shows the three types of volcanoes that Dr. Fryer discussed in her lecture. Add three or four key points about each type.

Volcano Types	Key Points
Volcano type: _____	
Volcano type: _____	
Volcano type: _____	

B Work in a small group. Take turns saying one key point about one type of volcano. Your group members should name the volcano type you are describing.

> **Example:** Student A: *This type of volcano makes a hole in the ground instead of a cone.*
> Student B: *That is a super volcano.*

Unit 1 Academic Vocabulary Review

This section reviews the vocabulary from Chapters 1 and 2. Some of the words that you needed to learn to understand the content of this unit are specific to its topics. Other words are more general. They appear across different academic fields and are extremely useful for all students to know. For a complete list of all the Academic Word List words in this book, see the Appendix on page 180.

A Read the sentences and fill in the blanks with a form of the word.

1. **affect (v), affected (adj):**
   Earthquakes can seriously _____ people living in crowded cities.

2. **alternative (n), alternating (adj):**
   Composite volcanoes have _____ layers of ash and lava.

3. **core (n), cored (adj):**
   The _____ of Earth is made of molten rock.

4. **create (v), creation (n):**
   A volcano in the middle of the ocean can _____ an island.

5. **energy (n), energetic (adj):**
   Scientists use special machines to measure the _____ of an earthquake.

6. **features (v), featured (adj):**
   Mars and Earth have similar land _____ .

7. **internal (adj), internalize (v):**
   The _____ part of a volcano includes a central channel called a vent.

8. **layer (n), layered (adj):**
   Earth's outer _____ is called the crust.

9. **structure (n), structural (adj):**
   The _____ of some volcanoes looks like a cone.

10. **percent (n), percentage (n):**
    Volcanoes make about 75 _____ of all the rocks on Earth.

11. **final (adj), finally (adv):**
    When the lava _____ cooled, it became hard like rock.

12. **lecture (n), lectured (v):**
    The instructor's _____ was about the history of Mt. Kilauea.

B Use the academic vocabulary from Step A above to answer the following questions in pairs or as a class.

Surface Features

1. How are Mars and Earth similar?
2. What is unique about the surface of Earth?
3. How do landforms change over time?

Earth's Structure

4. What are the main layers of Earth?
5. In what sense is Earth's structure "dynamic"?
6. How do moving plates affect Earth?

Volcanoes

7. What are three different kinds of volcanoes?
8. Why do volcanoes erupt?
9. What happens after an eruption?

Pangea

10. What was Pangea?
11. How did Pangea change over time?
12. What does this tell us about the future of Earth?

Oral Presentation

As a student, you may have the opportunity to participate in a poster session. In a poster session, you give your presentation to a small group of listeners and repeat your presentation many times.

1 Choose a topic

For this presentation, you will learn more about Earth's dynamic nature. Choose one of the topics from the chart below to research.

Top 10 Deadliest Earthquakes	Top 10 Famous Volcanoes
1556 Shaanxi, China	Mt. Vesuvius
1976 Tangshan, China	Krakatoa
2004 Indian Ocean Tsunami	Mt. St. Helens
1920 Haiyuan, China	Mt. Tambora
1923 Kanto, Japan	Mauna Loa
1948 Turkmenistan	Eyjafjallajokull
2008 Sichuan Province, China	Mt. Pelee
2005 Kashmir, Pakistan	Thera
1908 Messina, Italy	Nevado del Ruiz
1970 Chimbote, Peru	Mt. Pinatubo

2 Research your topic

Research your topic online. Find the following information about your topic:

- a map showing where the event (earthquake or volcanic eruption) happened
- the date of the earthquake or eruption
- the number of victims (people who died)
- other effects (on buildings, people, the environment, etc.)
- other interesting or surprising facts about the event

3 Prepare your poster

An effective poster is visually appealing and communicates information clearly to your audience. Follow these guidelines to make an effective poster:

- Do not use a lot of words. Avoid complete sentences and just use key words and headings.
- Organize the information on your poster so that it is easy for your audience to understand.
- Use pictures, charts, or other visuals to help your audience understand the information.
- Make the words and pictures on your poster large enough for the audience to read. Remember to leave some open space, too!

1 Use your poster effectively

During your poster session, a small group of listeners (3–5 people) will gather around the poster to hear about your topic. You can speak more casually than in a formal presentation situation, but you should still explain your topic slowly and clearly. Follow these guidelines to use your poster effectively:

- Stand next to your poster, not in front of it. **Do not read sentences from your poster**. Instead, make **eye contact** with your audience while you are speaking.
- When you want to draw your audience's attention to information on your poster, you can point to the poster and use expressions such as:

This is a picture of . . .　　　　　*This map shows . . .*

As you can see here . . .　　　　　*This graph illustrates . . .*

2 Focus on fluency and pace

After you finish giving your presentation once, a new group of listeners will come to your poster. Repeating your presentation many times will help you improve the fluency and pace of your speech.

Fluency refers to the smoothness of your speech. Try to speak in a smooth, continuous manner without stopping for long periods of time or repeating yourself too much. Also try to reduce fillers, such as "um," "ah," "er," "like," etc.

Pace refers to the speed of your speech. People usually speak faster when they give a presentation because they are nervous, but it is important to speak slowly enough for your listeners to understand. Try to speak a little slower than the pace you use for daily conversation. Also, pause briefly after finishing one section of your presentation and before starting the next section. This will give your listeners time to think about the information they just heard.

Interact with your audience

Because a poster session has an informal, small group format, it is a very good opportunity for the speaker and listeners to interact.

Your listeners may ask you questions during your presentation. Do not be surprised if they ask questions; just try your best to answer them, and then resume your speech. If you cannot understand a question, you can say, "I'm sorry, could you please repeat your question?"

After you finish your presentation, you can ask your listeners if they have any further questions. Here are some useful expressions:

Can I explain anything in more detail?
Is there anything that was unclear to you?
Do you have any questions about my poster?

Unit 2
Water on Earth

In this unit, you are going to learn about one of our most precious resources – water. Chapter 3 focuses on freshwater. It includes interviews with people who talk about the water supply in different countries around the world. The lecture is about the natural water cycle and some of the problems threatening Earth's water cycle today. Chapter 4 examines Earth's vast oceans. Two interviewees talk about their love of the ocean and water sports. The lecture describes some unique features of the ocean.

Contents

In Unit 2, you will listen to and speak about the following topics.

Chapter 3 Earth's Water Supply	Chapter 4 Earth's Oceans
Interview 1 Water in the United States **Interview 2** Water in Cambodia **Interview 3** Water in Cameroon **Lecture** Sources and Functions of Surface Water	**Interview 1** Adventure Under the Ocean **Interview 2** Surf's Up **Lecture** One World Ocean

Skills

In Unit 2, you will practice the following skills.

L Listening Skills	**S** Speaking Skills
Listening for opinions Listening for details Listening for specific information Listening for main ideas Expressing likes and dislikes Thinking critically about the topic Listening for signal words and phrases Personalizing the topic	Examining graphic material Examining a map Applying what you have learned Predicting the content Considering related information Sharing your opinion Retelling what you have heard Thinking creatively about the topic Building background knowledge on the topic
V Vocabulary Skills	**N** Note Taking Skills
Reading and thinking about the topic Building background vocabulary Guessing vocabulary from context	Using symbols and abbreviations Using bullets and brackets to organize your notes Rewriting your notes after a lecture Using handouts to help you take notes Focusing on the conclusion Making test questions from your notes

Learning Outcomes

Prepare and **deliver** an oral presentation about daily water usage

Chapter 3
Earth's Water Supply

Look at the photographs and answer the questions with a partner.

1. How are these people using water? Describe the activities in each photo.

2. How do you use water in your daily life?

3. Why is it important to use water carefully?

1 Getting Started

In this section, you are going to read about Earth's water and the natural cycle it follows. You will begin to think about the different forms water can take and all the places it can be found on our planet.

1 Reading and thinking about the topic Ⓥ Ⓢ

A Read the following passage.

All of Earth's water is the same age as the planet itself – 4.6 billion years old. No new water has been added to Earth, and no water has been lost. This means that the water you drink is billions of years old! Don't be alarmed – Earth's water supply is constantly being renewed and refreshed. In a process called the *hydrologic cycle*, it changes from liquid to gas, and then back again. The cycle starts when liquid water evaporates, or changes into a gas. The vapor rises into the atmosphere and forms clouds. Then rain falls from the clouds onto land, where it collects in lakes and rivers. Rivers take the water back to the oceans, and the cycle begins again.

Most of Earth's water – about 97 percent – is in the oceans. Only three percent of Earth's water is found in other places, including lakes and rivers, ice, groundwater, and in the atmosphere. This three percent also includes the water found in plants and in the bodies of humans and animals. Earth's water is constantly moving and changing form, but it never goes away.

B Answer the following questions according to the information in the passage.

1. How has the amount of water on Earth changed since the planet was formed 4.6 billion years ago?
2. Name at least six places where water exists on Earth as it passes through the hydrologic cycle.

C Read the following questions and share your answers with a partner.

1. Where do you see water every day? Make a list of all the places.
2. Life on Earth could not exist without water. What are some ways that plants, animals, and humans use water?

2 Building background vocabulary Ⓥ

A Read the list. The words name different forms of water. Each form of water is either a gas, liquid, or solid. Write each word in the correct column of the chart.

| cloud | lake | rain | snow | waterfall |
| ice | ocean | river | steam | |

GAS	LIQUID	SOLID

B Look at the pictures of the different forms that water can take in nature. Write the correct words from Step A on page 44.

1. _____   2. _____   3. _____

4. _____   5. _____   6. _____

C Listen to the following sounds. As you listen, write the form of water in Step B that makes each sound.

1. _____   4. _____

2. _____   5. _____

3. _____   6. _____

D Compare your answers to Step C with a partner. Then discuss the following questions.

1. Have you seen places like those in the pictures in Step B? Where did you see them? Tell your partner about your experience in each place.

2. In addition to the places in the pictures in Step B, where else can you see water in nature?

2 Real-Life Voices

In this section, you are going to hear four people talk about access to water in three different countries: the United States, Cambodia, and Cameroon.

BEFORE THE INTERVIEWS

Examining graphic material ⓢ

> Scientific data is often presented in graphic form, so it is important to practice reading and understanding graphs and charts.

A The chart below compares water use in different countries. Work with a partner. Look at the chart and then discuss the questions that follow it.

Water use at the beginning of the twenty-first century		
Country	Total water use (km^3 per year)	Water use per person (m^3 per year)
Brazil	58.07	297
Cameroon	0.29	34
Japan	88.43	696
Mexico	79.80	721
Turkey	40.10	530
United States	482.20	1,518

Source: The World's Water, Peter H. Gleick, Pacific Institute (2010)

1. Which country uses the most water? Which country uses the least water?
2. What are some possible reasons for the great difference in water usage around the world?
3. Does any of the information in the chart surprise you? Explain your answer.

B As you learned in Step A, the United States uses more water per person than any other country. How are Americans using all that water? Look at the graph below and fill in the blanks. Use the phrases below.

Domestic Use (use by individuals and families at home)

Industrial Use (use by factories and manufacturers)

Agricultural Use (use by farmers to grow crops)

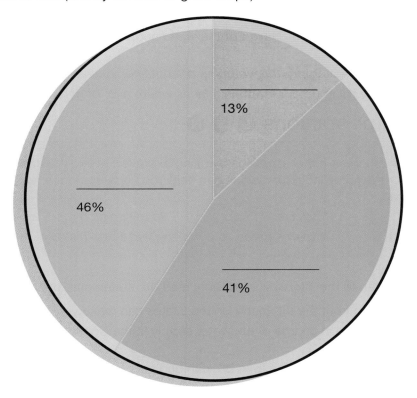

13%

46%

41%

C Check your answers to Step B on the bottom of page 48. Discuss them with a partner.

Here are some words and expressions from the interview with Gina, printed in **bold** and given in the context in which you will hear them. They are followed by definitions.

. . . we don't have to worry about **access** to water: *ability to use or get something*

. . . you can't drink the **tap water**: *water from a faucet*

. . . some people think that there are **pollutants** in their drinking water: *things that make air or water dirty and possibly dangerous*

. . . the people who are **in charge of** the water supply: *responsible for the care or supervision of*

Because of its **packaging**: *the wrapping or container in which something is sold*

. . . are quickly filling up our **landfills**: *places where a lot of garbage is buried*

Listening for opinions Ⓛ Ⓢ Ⓝ

Speakers often present their opinions by using expressions like the ones below. Listening for the following expressions can help you understand a speaker's opinion about a topic.

I think . . .	I believe . . .	In my opinion . . .
I feel (like) . . .	It seems to me . . .	The way I see it is . . .

A Before you listen to the interview with Gina, read the statements below.

_____ **1.** Drinking from the tap in the United States can make you sick.

_____ **2.** The people in charge of the water supply in the United States make sure the water is safe.

_____ **3.** The water where Gina lives is clean and safe to drink.

_____ **4.** Tap water is not as good as bottled water.

_____ **5.** Bottled water is bad for the environment.

_____ **6.** If we use fewer plastic bottles for water, it will help our environment.

🔊 **B** Now listen to the interview. Pay attention to the expressions Gina uses when she states her opinions. Check (✓) all of the statements in Step A that Gina agrees with.

Answers to Step B on page 47: Domestic Use:
13%; Industrial Use: 46%; Agricultural Use: 41%

C Work with a partner. Compare your answers to Step B and then discuss the following questions. Use some of the expressions in the box on page 48 in your discussion.

1. Does the drinking water where you live taste good?
2. Do you prefer drinking tap water, filtered water, or bottled water? Explain your answer.
3. Is bottled water bad for our environment? Explain.

INTERVIEW 2   Water in Cambodia

Here are some words and expressions from the interview with Lara and David, printed in **bold** and given in the context in which you will hear them. They are followed by definitions.

. . . in the **capital city**: *the city where the government of a country, state, etc., is officially located*

Thousands of children die from **water-borne** illnesses: *carried by or grown in water*

People drink mostly **surface water**: *water found above the ground, such as in lakes, ponds, or rivers*

. . . the surface water contains. . .? . . . **Feces**: *solid waste from the bodies of animals or humans*

Listing for details ⓛ

One way to deepen your understanding of recorded material is to connect details and main ideas. Doing that will help you understand the relationship between ideas, facts, and statistics.

A Work with a partner. Read some of the problems that Lara and David discuss. Where do you think people experience these problems? Write *capital city*, *countryside*, or *whole country* next to each one.

1. _____ People drink mostly surface water.
2. _____ People don't have enough money to buy wood to boil the water.
3. _____ The water has feces in it.
4. _____ People have to buy water from trucks.
5. _____ Thousands of children die from water-borne illnesses every year.
6. _____ The water is very thick, sort of a tea color.

B Listen to the interview with Lara and David. As you listen, check your answers to Step A.

Here are some words and expressions from the interview with Seónagh, printed in bold and given in the context in which you will hear them. They are followed by definitions.

That's what **made sense** to me: *was a good idea; showed good judgment*

It's just **heartbreaking**: *very sad and upsetting*

Water is something that you need to **survive**: *be able to live*

Are people less **wasteful** of water: *tending to use much more than necessary*

Water is a **metaphor** for life: *a kind of comparison*

Listening for specific information Ⓛ Ⓢ Ⓝ

Sometimes textbooks or instructors provide questions to help you focus on specific information in a listening passage or lecture. Preview the questions before you listen so that you know what information to listen for.

🔊 **A** Read the questions below before you listen to the interview with Seónagh. Then listen and take notes on the answers.

1. How long did Seónagh live in Cameroon?

_____

2. What did she do to make sure that she did not get sick from the water?

_____

3. Why do some people in Cameroon have to travel very far to get water?

_____

4. What is Seónagh's opinion about the people in Cameroon?

_____

5. How did she change after living in Cameroon?

_____

🔊 **B** A simile is a way of comparing two things using the words *as* or *like*, for example: *The water is **as toxic as poison**; Drinking contaminated water is **like drinking poison**.* Metaphors, on the other hand, make a stronger comparison, often by using a form of the verb *be*: *For young children, contaminated water **is poison***. Listen again to the last part of the interview with Seónagh. Circle the similes and metaphors.

Water comes from Earth and flows across Earth. It's like blood. In some cultures, water is seen as the blood of Earth. I think of it that way. The Earth is like a living thing. All the plants and animals are parts of the Earth's "body." And everything is connected by water. To me, water is a metaphor for life.

C Work with a partner. Compare your answers in Steps A and B. Then think of your own similes and metaphors for water. Share them with the class.

AFTER THE INTERVIEWS

1 Examining a map ⓢ

A Look at the map below. It shows areas of the world that are experiencing water stress (demand for water is high compared to the supply). Discuss the questions that follow in a small group.

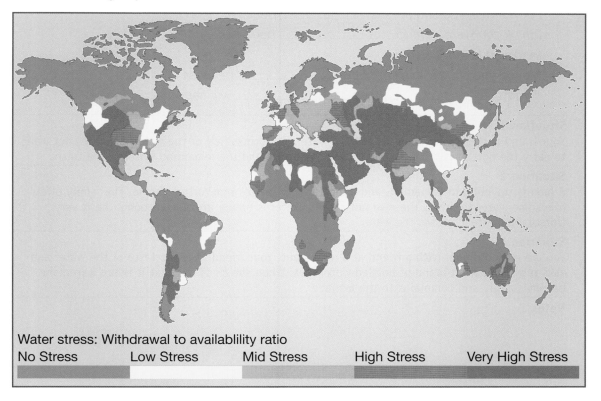

Water stress: Withdrawal to availablility ratio

No Stress   Low Stress   Mid Stress   High Stress   Very High Stress

B Why do some areas of the world not have enough water? Think about what you heard in the interviews with Gina, Lara, David, and Seónagh and brainstorm possible causes of water stress.

C Have you ever traveled to a country that was experiencing water stress? Describe your experience.

2 Applying what you have learned Ⓢ

> Finding ways to apply what you have learned is a good way to deepen your
> understanding of a topic.

A Work in a small group. Choose one of the situations below and imagine how you would
respond. What would you say to the person or people? What would you do?
Make notes. Use the expressions below to help you.

I don't think you should _____ *because . . .*

I think you were right to _____ *because . . .*

In this situation, I would . . .

Maybe you should think about _____ *because . . .*

If you _____ *, then* _____ *will happen.*

Situation 1   Your friend is thirsty and buys a bottle of water. She drinks half of the water. She does not want to carry the bottle with her, so she throws the bottle and the remaining water in the trash.
Situation 2   A man is traveling in Cameroon, and a local family invites him to their home. The family offers him some water to drink. The man notices the water is brown in color. Although he is very thirsty, he politely refuses the water.
Situation 3   You are eating dinner with a friend at a restaurant. Your friend likes the taste of the water and asks the server what brand of bottled water it is. When she finds out that it is tap water, she becomes angry and complains to the manager.
Notes

B Share your group's ideas about the situation you chose with the class.

3 In Your Own Voice

In this section, you are going to learn about some proverbs and idiomatic expressions related to water. Then you will share other water-related proverbs that you know.

A Read the proverbs and idiomatic expressions related to water. Match them with their meanings below. Then compare your answers with a partner's.

_____ **1.** You can lead a horse to water, but you can't make it drink.

_____ **2.** Blood is thicker than water.

_____ **3.** Don't wash your dirty clothes in public.

_____ **4.** Don't throw the baby out with the bath water.

_____ **5.** That's water under the bridge.

_____ **6.** Still water runs deep.

_____ **7.** He's in hot water.

_____ **8.** He has his head in the clouds.

_____ **9.** He's a big fish in a small pond.

_____ **10.** You can never enter the same river twice.

a. He has an important position, but in a small group or organization.

b. Don't discuss personal problems with people outside your home.

c. You can never have exactly the same relationship or experience again.

d. Family is more important than friendships or other relationships.

e. Quiet people often have strong thoughts, feelings, and insights.

f. He's in trouble.

g. He is not being realistic.

h. If you have to make an important change, keep what is good.

i. You can tell people what's good for them, but you can't make them do it.

j. We had a problem, but it was in the past and we can forget about it.

B Work with a partner. Do you know any other proverbs related to water? Share them with your partner. If you know water-related proverbs from another language, explain them to your partner in English.

4 Academic Listening and Note Taking

In this section, you are going to hear and take notes on a two-part lecture by Martha McDaniel, the director of a nature preserve. In her lecture, "Sources and Functions of Surface Water," Ms. McDaniel will introduce the sources and functions of surface water. Then she will discuss some current threats to Earth's freshwater supply.

BEFORE THE LECTURE

1 Predicting the content Ⓢ

> Thinking about the topic and trying to predict what you are going to hear will help your listening comprehension.

A In the lecture, Ms. McDaniel explains how freshwater gets on the surface of Earth. Think about what you already know about the water cycle, and then number the pictures in order from 1 to 4.

B Ms. McDaniel will also talk about different forms and quantities of water on Earth. Predict the percentages for each form of water below.

    _____ **1.** freshwater   **a.** less than 3%

    _____ **2.** ice   **b.** 97%

    _____ **3.** drinkable water   **c.** 3%

    _____ **4.** saltwater   **d.** less than 1%

C Compare your answers to Steps A and B with a partner's. Then check your answers on the bottom of page 56. Were your predictions correct?

2 Using symbols and abbreviations Ⓝ Ⓛ

To take notes during a lecture, you have to write a lot of information very quickly. One way to save time is to use symbols and abbreviations instead of writing out each word.

Symbols are pictures or marks that represent words. Here are some common symbols:

+ or &	and	⟶	leads to, causes
%	percent	"	ditto (same as above)
∴	therefore	#	number
=	equals, is	↑, ↓	increase, decrease
≠	not, not the same as	>, <	more than, less than

Abbreviations are short forms of a word. Ways to make abbreviations include:
• Writing only the first syllable (sometimes with the first letter of the next syllable)
• Writing only the first letter or two of each syllable (sometimes with a slash)
• Writing the word without vowels

ex	example	ppl	people
b/c	because	yr	year
w/	with	esp	especially
w/o	without	usu	usually
imp	important	smts	sometimes

A Study the symbols and abbreviations. Then match them with the words on the right. Think about how each abbreviation was created.

_____ **1.** E
_____ **2.** surf
_____ **3.** w/
_____ **4.** %
_____ **5.** fr
_____ **6.** H_2O
_____ **7.** =
_____ **8.** +
_____ **9.** ppl
_____ **10.** anim

a. surface
b. fresh
c. animals
d. with
e. and, as well as
f. people
g. Earth
h. is, is called
i. percent, percentage
j. water

🔊 **B** Watch or listen to excerpts from the introduction to the lecture. As you listen, take
🎥 notes using symbols and abbreviations. Remember to also use telegraphic language.

1. Most of E's _____

2. _____ = salt _____; _____ fr H_2O

3. Of all fresh H_2O: _____ only _____

4. _____ = drinking _____

C Compare your notes with a partner. What new information about water did you learn in the introduction?

1 Guessing vocabulary from context ⓥ

A The following sentences and phrases contain important vocabulary from Part 1 of the lecture. Work with a partner. Using the context and your knowledge of related words, take turns guessing the meanings of the words in **bold**.

_____ **1.** . . . there is **plenty** of water on Earth . . .

_____ **2.** Today I will talk about this amazing, **precious** resource.

_____ **3.** . . . much of the water **sinks** into the ground and becomes groundwater.

_____ **4.** Rivers carry **nutrients** and spread them over the land as they flow.

_____ **5.** As a result, most land near rivers is rich and **fertile**.

_____ **6.** Of course, farmers also need to give their **crops** freshwater every day . . .

_____ **7.** Water is used in **industry** . . .

_____ **8.** Water is used . . . for **transportation** . . .

B Work with a partner. Match the bold terms in the sentences in Step A with their definitions below. If necessary, use a dictionary to check your answers.

a. (of land) having the nutrients to produce healthy plants

b. goes down below the surface

c. the business of making products, especially in factories

d. a system for carrying people or goods from one place to another

e. more than enough

f. substances that help plants and animals live and grow

g. very important; very valuable

h. plants that are not wild but are grown by people

Answers to Steps A and B on page 55:
top row, left to right: 4, 2
bottom row, left to right: 3, 1
1 c; 2 a; 3 d; 4 b

2 Using symbols and abbreviations Ⓝ Ⓛ

A When taking notes, it's a good idea to use abbreviations. Doing that will help you to be a fast and efficient note taker. A common technique for abbreviating words is to omit vowels. One way to abbreviate *ocean*, therefore, would be *ocn*. Another way is to shorten a word. *Biology*, for example, could be abbreviated as *bio*. There is no "correct" way to use abbreviations in your notes, as long as you can understand them afterward. Practice by creating abbreviations for the words listed below. You will hear these words in the next lecture.

Word	Abbreviation	Word	Abbreviation
enjoyment		river	
flow		saltwater	
freshwater		stream	
ground		surface	
industry		transportation	

B Look at the outline below. Think about what kind of information you need in order to fill in the blanks.

I. Where does fr. H$_2$O come from?
   A. Rain + snow falls ⟶ sinks into _____
   B. If _____ is full of H$_2$O, then stays on _____
   C. Small flow of surf water = _____
   D. If combine, become bigger = _____
   C. May form pond / lake, or flow to ocn.

II. Functions of fresh H$_2$O
   A. _____ carry nutrients + minerals ∴ nearby land rich + fertile
     Farmers also have to give crops _____
   B. Daily tasks, ex. washing dishes + clothes, cleaning, bathing
   C. _____
   D. _____
   E. Playing + _____
   F. *most important = _____ for humans + _____
     Without _____ life on Earth couldn't exist

C Watch or listen to Part 1 of the lecture. As you listen to the introduction, refer back to your notes in Step B on page 55. Then complete the notes for the rest of Part 1, above, using symbols and abbreviations.

D Work with a partner. Compare your answers. Your symbols and abbreviations do not have to be exactly the same, as long as you understand your own notes.

1 Guessing vocabulary from context

A The following items contain important vocabulary from Part 2 of the lecture. Work with a partner. Using the context and your knowledge of related words, take turns guessing the meanings of the words in **bold**.

_____ **1.** Unfortunately, there are many problems **threatening** Earth's freshwater supply today.

_____ **2.** When we cover the earth with **concrete** . . .

_____ **3.** **Pollution** also affects our water supply.

_____ **4.** Pollution comes from many sources: Factories, human waste, and **fertilizers** are just a few examples.

_____ **5.** Water is our most important natural **resource**.

_____ **6.** All countries around the world need to **cooperate** in order to stop pollution . . .

B Work with your partner. Match the bold terms in the sentences in Step A with their definitions below. If necessary, use a dictionary to check your answers.

a. a basic material that comes from nature

b. harmful things that are put into a natural environment

c. something people add to soil to help plants grow

d. a hard, rocklike substance used for building

e. work together

f. presenting danger or risk

2 Using bullets and brackets to organize your notes

Bulleted lists and brackets can help in organizing your notes. Bulleted lists can be used to organize topics or details. Brackets can be used to summarize group items in a list or draw a conclusion.

A Look at the sample notes from Part 2 of the lecture. Use the notes to explain the first threat to Earth's freshwater supply to a partner.

Threats to E's fresh H_2O supply
1. Loss of nat envir
   • bldgs, roads, pking lots
   • land cov'd w/ concrete
   • land development affects H_2O supply in negative way
} Affect qual of fr H_2O

B Now watch or listen to Part 2 of the lecture. As you listen, complete the notes using bullets and brackets.

2. _____
   • many sources, ex. factories, hum waste + fert
   • poll in air: _____ falls to E, enters H_2O supply
   • trash enters strm or riv

3. Overuse by humans
   • H_2O cannot ↑ but pop ↑ every yr
   • millions more ppl → _____ → need for more _____ → more farming → more _____ for _____

CONCLUSION
   • Ppl can't live more than a few days w/o H_2O
   • Ppl must learn not to waste H_2O
   • All countries must coop to stop _____

C Compare your notes with a partner.

1 Rewriting your notes after a lecture

Rewriting your notes after a lecture helps you understand and remember the content. You should do this within 24 hours of the lecture, while the information is still fresh in your mind.

A Rewrite your notes from the lecture. As you rewrite, check (✓) each item in the list below.

Checklist for rewriting notes
Reorganize notes so that the main ideas and important supporting details are clear.
Write notes neatly so that you can read all the information.
Add information you did not have time to write down during the lecture.
Change abbreviations and symbols back into words, especially if you think you might forget their meaning.
If you notice that information is missing from your notes, choose a strategy from Step B, below, to help you.

B If you did not understand some information in a lecture, use one of the following strategies.

- Guess from context: Look at the information before and after the part that you did not understand and make a logical guess.
- Use your textbook: If the lecture refers to a reading assignment in a textbook, look for the missing information in your book.
- Ask your classmate: "What did you hear about _____?" or "I missed the part about _____ . Did you get it?"
- Ask the lecturer: "Excuse me, can you tell me what you said about _____ ?" or "I'm sorry, I missed the part about _____ . Would you please repeat it?"

2 Considering related information Ⓢ Ⓥ

A Read the following passage about Earth's water supply. Discuss the meaning of the reading as a class.

There should be enough freshwater to meet the needs of Earth's people. However, one in six people does not get enough clean water to meet their daily needs. The United Nations has set a goal to cut this number in half. To achieve this goal, people everywhere must learn to conserve water at an individual, local, national, and global level.

B Choose one question below. Write all of the answers you can think of. To get more information, talk to people outside of your class or do research on the Internet.

1. Individual action: What can an individual do to conserve water?

2. National action: What can a country do to conserve water?

3. Global action: What can an international group do to encourage people all over the world to conserve water?

C Form a group with the people in your class who chose the same question you did. Share your ideas with the group members.

Chapter 4
Earth's Oceans

1. Describe the plants and animals in the picture. Use adjectives and other descriptive words.

2. Have you ever been to the ocean? Do you go there often? Talk about a place by the sea that you know.

3. What feelings do you get when you think about the ocean? Describe your feelings to a classmate.

1 Getting Started

In this section, you are going to read about features of the world's oceans and the important roles they play on Earth.

1 Reading and thinking about the topic

A Read the following passage.

Earth has four main oceans: the Pacific, the Atlantic, the Indian, and the Arctic. Many scientists count a fifth ocean, called the Southern Ocean. In addition, Earth has seas, bays, and gulfs, which are smaller bodies of saltwater partly surrounded by land. Although these bodies of water are in different areas of the world, water flows constantly from one area to the next, mixing and forming one "world ocean."

As you can see in the map below, there is much more ocean than land on our planet. The oceans cover 71 percent of Earth's surface. They also provide a huge living space for plants and animals. In fact, oceans make up 99 percent of Earth's total livable space. The oceans affect weather and climate and are an important source of food and energy. They are also important for commerce, transportation, and recreation. The world ocean is so big and deep that scientists have explored only 5 percent of it. Who knows what we will find under the water in the future?

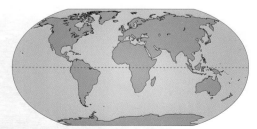

Northern hemisphere
61 percent ocean

Southern hemisphere
80 percent ocean

B Answer the following questions according to the information in the passage.

1. What is the difference between an ocean and a sea, bay, or gulf?
2. Why is "world ocean" a good name for all of Earth's oceans, seas, bays, and gulfs?
3. What do each of the following percentages from the passage represent? 5%, 71%, 99%

C Read the following questions and share your answers with a partner.

1. Is there an ocean near your hometown? If so, how does it affect life there (for example, the weather, people's hobbies, jobs, etc.)?
2. Most of the ocean has never been explored. What do you think scientists might find in the ocean in the future?

2 Expressing likes and dislikes 🄻 🅂

Speakers have different ways of saying what they like and don't like.
Here are some expressions you may hear:

Like: *I [really] like . . .*   Dislike: *I don't [really] like . . .*
       I enjoy . . .   *I don't care for . . .*
       I love . . .   *I hate . . .*
       I'm crazy about . . .   *I can't stand . . .*

A Look at the different activities shown below. Write the correct vocabulary word for the activity under each picture.

1. _____   2. _____   3. _____   4. _____   5. _____

B Now listen to several people talk about the activities in Step A. Write the activity you hear and circle each speaker's opinion about it.

1. _____ Like / Dislike   4. _____ Like / Dislike
2. _____ Like / Dislike   5. _____ Like / Dislike
3. _____ Like / Dislike

C Work with a partner and compare your answers to Steps A and B. Then think of two more activities that can be done at the ocean. Write them in spaces provided below.

_____   _____

2 Real-Life Voices

In this section, you are going to hear two people talk about their favorite ocean activities: diving and surfing.

BEFORE THE INTERVIEWS

1 Sharing your opinion Ⓢ Ⓥ

A In the interviews, the speakers use the adjectives below to describe the ocean and diving. Read through the list of words with a partner. If there are words you do not know, look them up in a dictionary.

boring	interesting	quiet	surprising
calm	peaceful	relaxing	threatening

B In your opinion, which three adjectives in Step A best describe the ocean? Circle them. Then add two more adjectives of your own that describe it.

C In a small group, share your answers to Step B. For each word that you circle, explain your choice by using this expression.

I think the ocean is _____ because . . .

D In your group, vote on the three words that best describe the ocean. Write your answers here.

_____ _____ _____

2 Predicting the content Ⓛ

A In the next section, you are going to hear interviews with Edmund, a diver, and Tomoki, a surfer. Read the following excerpts from the interviews with a partner. Try to predict which speaker will say each statement. Write *E* (Edmund) or *T* (Tomoki) next to each statement.

    _____ **1.** It feels like you're sliding over the wave . . . like you're flying through the water.

    _____ **2.** The ocean is very quiet and calm . . . you can just sit there and look at the fish.

    _____ **3.** I often see something or find something interesting.

    _____ **4.** Although there were a couple times when I felt scared. . . .

    _____ **5.** You really feel the power of nature, the power of the waves in your whole body.

B After you have listened to both interviews, return to this task and check your predictions. Were they correct?

INTERVIEW 1   Adventure Under the Ocean

Here are some words and expressions from the interview with Edmund, printed in **bold** and given in the context in which you will hear them. They are followed by definitions.

When I was younger, I wanted to be a marine **biologist**: *a scientist who studies plants and animals that live in the ocean*

Then when I was in high school, I **got certified** in scuba diving: *got a certificate showing completion of a class, course, or program*

When you dive with your equipment, your **tank**, how long can you stay underwater?: *a container for holding oxygen*

. . . I was out diving and a **sea horse** swam by: *a small fish with a horse-like head and a bottom half that curls downward*

So the ocean never feels **threatening** to you at all?: *causing alarm or a feeling of danger*

A few times **an eel** has hit me while I was diving: *a long, snake-like fish*

. . . I looked up and saw two huge **fins**: *thin, wing-shaped parts of fish that help them swim*

. . . I started **panicking** because the fins were bigger than me: *feeling out of control and acting out of fear*

Retelling what you have heard Ⓢ Ⓛ

A Look at the pictures below. With a partner, discuss what you see and what you think is happening in each picture.

1

2

3

4

🔊 **B** Listen to the interview with Edmund. Take notes as Edmund talks about each situation shown in Step A.

C Work in a small group. Take turns retelling Edmund's stories about what he found and saw when he was scuba diving. Use your notes and the pictures in Step A to tell each story.

INTERVIEW 2 Surf's Up

Here are some words and expressions from the interview with Tomoki, printed in **bold** and given in the context in which you will hear them. They are followed by definitions.

> . . . I just thought I'd **give it a shot**: *try something*
>
> I think physically, you need to be **fit**: *healthy and strong*
>
> . . . you need to have **good balance**: *a state in which the body is steady*
>
> We say that the surface is **choppy** or clean: *forming short, broken waves*
>
> The waves are moving your **entire** body through the ocean: *whole or complete*

1 Listening for main ideas Ⓛ Ⓢ

A The following questions are about the main ideas in the interview with Tomoki. Read the questions before you listen.

1. Why did Tomoki start surfing?

_____ He had been interested in the sport since his childhood.

_____ His friend gave him a surfboard.

_____ As a child, he spent every summer at the beach, playing in the water.

2. Why does Tomoki love surfing?

_____ He loves being in the water.   _____ He loves being in the sun.

_____ Surfing is challenging.   _____ Surfing is easy.

_____ The ocean is beautiful.   _____ Surfing is unique.

3. According to Tomoki, what does a person need to surf well?

_____ physical fitness   _____ very big waves

_____ good balance   _____ strong wind

_____ a good surfboard   _____ a clean ocean surface

🔊 **B** Listen to the interview with Tomoki. Check (✓) all of his responses to the questions in Step A.

C Work with a partner and compare answers.

2 Thinking critically about the topic Ⓛ Ⓢ

As a student, you will often need to think critically about a topic. This means you must do more than restate what you hear and read. You must think carefully about the information and analyze it.

A Read the statement below. Circle the word that you think best completes the sentence.

Edmund and Tomoki think that humans (can / cannot) control the ocean.

🔊 **B** Listen to the last part of the interviews with Edmund and Tomoki again. Check your answer in Step A. Explain your answer using information from the interviews.

C Now complete the sentence with your own opinion. Explain your opinion to a partner.

I think that humans (can / cannot) control the ocean.

Thinking creatively about the topic ⓢ ⓥ

> Using your imagination to think about a topic can give you new ideas and insights. Thinking creatively is also a good way to practice new vocabulary and demonstrate your understanding of the topic.

A Read the two diary entries below. Which one was written by Edmund? Which one was written by Tomoki? Write the correct name for each diary entry.

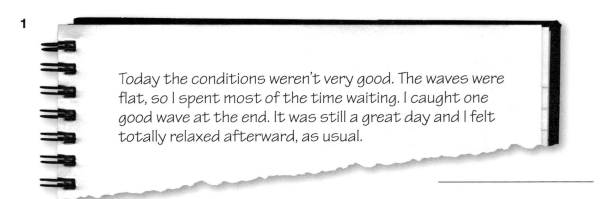

1

Today the conditions weren't very good. The waves were flat, so I spent most of the time waiting. I caught one good wave at the end. It was still a great day and I felt totally relaxed afterward, as usual.

_____

2

This morning I saw a whitetip shark just outside of the bay. It wasn't too big, probably still a baby. I followed it for about 50 meters before I lost it. The light was so good today! Good thing I had brought my camera with me.

_____

B Imagine that you are Edmund or Tomoki after a day of diving or surfing. On a separate piece of paper, write a diary entry. Describe what you saw and how you felt in the ocean. Use new words and phrases from the interviews. The phrases below may also help you.

Today I spent . . . hours in the ocean.
The conditions were . . . / The waves were . . . / The wind was . . . / The water was . . . / . . .
I saw . . . It was amazing / scary / fascinating / boring / . . .
I felt relaxed / scared / happy / . . .

C Read your diary entry to a partner.

3 In Your Own Voice

In this section, you and your classmates are going to share experiences and opinions about Earth's oceans.

Personalizing the topic ⓛ ⓢ

A Walk around the classroom and ask your classmates the questions below. Write the name of the person who answers the question in the box and take notes on the answer. Try to have a different person answer each question.

Please tell me about a good experience you have had at the ocean. Name: _____	Describe a movie you have seen that is related to the ocean. Name: _____	What do you think is the biggest threat to Earth's oceans today? Name: _____
Describe a story you have heard about a mythical (not real) creature that lives in the ocean or sea. Name: _____	In your opinion, what are the most important resources that humans get from the ocean? Name: _____	Describe the most beautiful beach you have been to. Name: _____
In your opinion, what is the most interesting animal that lives in the ocean? What makes it interesting? Name: _____	Please tell me about your favorite water sport. Name: _____	Please tell me about a scary experience you have had at the ocean. Name: _____

B Work in a small group. Take turns explaining some of the answers you got. Then choose the most interesting answer in your group and share it with the class.

4 Academic Listening and Note Taking

In this section, you are going to hear a two-part lecture by Dr. Glen Jackson, a professor who teaches ocean science. The title of the lecture is "One World Ocean." In his lecture, Dr. Jackson will introduce Earth's oceans and describe their different layers.

BEFORE THE LECTURE

1 Building background knowledge on the topic ⓢ

A In this task, you are going to learn some facts about Earth's five oceans. Work with a partner.

Student A, look ONLY at Box A and fill in the missing information.

Student B, look ONLY at Box B (page 71) and fill in the missing information.

B Take turns checking your answers with your partner. Your partner will tell you if you are right or wrong. Here is an example.

A I think the Pacific Ocean is the largest ocean.

B That's correct. OK, I think the Indian Ocean is the smallest ocean.

A Sorry, that's not right. The Arctic Ocean is the smallest.

Box A

> Fill in each blank with the correct ocean: Pacific, Atlantic, Indian, Arctic, or Southern.
>
> **1.** The _____ Ocean is almost completely surrounded by land.
>
> **2.** The Marianas Trench, the world's deepest place, is located in the Pacific Ocean.
>
> **3.** The currents in the _____ Ocean change direction during the year, which causes monsoons (strong winds and heavy rains).
>
> **4.** The Atlantic Ocean is the least salty ocean because many rivers run into it.
>
> **5.** The _____ Ocean is sometimes called the Antarctic Ocean.
>
> **6.** The Southern Ocean surrounds the coldest, windiest place on Earth.
>
> **7.** The _____ Ocean has more water than all of the other oceans combined.
>
> **8.** The Atlantic Ocean is slowly growing larger because of plate tectonics.

Box B

Fill in each blank with the correct ocean: Pacific, Atlantic, Indian, Arctic, or Southern.

1. The Arctic Ocean is almost completely surrounded by land.

2. The Marianas Trench, the world's deepest place, is located in the _____ Ocean.

3. The currents in the Indian Ocean change direction during the year, which causes monsoons (strong winds and heavy rains).

4. The _____ Ocean is the least salty ocean because many rivers run into it.

5. The Southern Ocean is sometimes called the Antarctic Ocean.

6. The _____ Ocean surrounds the coldest, windiest place on Earth.

7. The Pacific Ocean has more water than all of the other oceans combined.

8. The _____ Ocean is slowly growing larger because of plate tectonics.

C Discuss any answers you got wrong with your partner and talk about any additional information you know about Earth's oceans.

2 Listening for signal words and phrases

Good lecturers use *signal words and phrases* to help listeners follow and understand a lecture. Signal words and phrases show the organization of a lecture. They also give information about the relationships among ideas in a lecture.

Introducing an example	*for instance / for example*
Emphasizing	*in fact / of course / clearly*
Introducing a cause	*because / since / due to*
Introducing an effect	*as a result / consequently / therefore*
Comparing	*(just) like / similarly / in the same way*
Contrasting	*however / in contrast / on the other hand*
Referring to background information	*as you (already) know*
Referring to information mentioned earlier	*as I (just) said / again*

A The signal words and phrases below are used by Dr. Jackson in the lecture. Find each word in the box on page 71 and write down its function.

However _____

Therefore _____

As I just said _____

Consequently _____

For example _____

B Work with a partner. Read the following sentences from the lecture and try to predict which signal word from Step A completes each sentence.

1. Some people say that there is one more ocean, called the Southern Ocean . . . (*However / Due to*), not all scientists agree that the Southern Ocean is a separate ocean basin.

2. The sun heats the seawater of this upper level. (*For instance / Therefore*), the surface layer is sometimes called the "sunlit zone."

3. The biggest difference between the surface layer and the middle layer is the temperature of the water. (*Consequently / As I just said*), the surface layer is relatively warm, with an average temperature of 17 degrees Celsius.

4. Sunlight becomes much weaker below the sunlit zone, so no plants can grow in the middle layer. (*Consequently / As you know*), most of the animals living in this layer have to swim up to the surface layer to find food.

5. The animals that live here have to adapt to be able to live in this cold and dark environment. (*Incidentally / For example*), many fish in the midnight zone do not have eyes.

🔊 📹 **C** Compare and discuss your answers with a partner. Then watch or listen to the sentences from the lecture and make corrections if necessary.

1 Guessing vocabulary from context Ⓥ

A The items below contain important vocabulary from Part 1 of the lecture. Work with a partner. Using the context and your knowledge of related words, take turns trying to guess the meanings of the words in **bold**.

_____ **1.** . . . the northern **hemisphere**, which is the top half of Earth, . . .

_____ **2.** Less than the southern hemisphere, but still **quite a bit**.

_____ **3.** . . . we can think of it as one world ocean, which is divided into four main ocean **basins.**

_____ **4.** Here we have the Atlantic Ocean, which **stretches** between Europe and Africa, over here, and the Americas.

_____ **5.** . . . we have the Indian Ocean, which is easy to remember because it **surrounds** the country of India.

_____ **6.** . . . we also have the Arctic Ocean, which is the smallest and **shallowest** ocean.

_____ **7. Density** has to do with "heaviness" . . .

B Work with your partner. Match the bold terms in the sentences in Step A with their definitions below. If necessary, use a dictionary to check your answers.

a. areas of land that are lower in the center than at the edges

b. the weight of a particular amount of something

c. circles or covers the area around something

d. spreads out over a large area

e. the least deep; having the least distance from surface to bottom

f. one half of Earth, either the northern half or the southern half

g. a lot

2 Using handouts to help you take notes Ⓝ Ⓛ Ⓢ

Sometimes a lecturer will give you a handout to help you understand the lecture better. When a lecturer refers to a handout, you can do any of the following:

• Highlight or circle parts that the lecturer discusses.

• Mark information that you do not understand or that you want to ask questions about.

• Write down additional information that you hear.

A The handouts on pages 74 and 76 accompany Dr. Jackson's lecture. Work with a partner. Look at the handouts and try to predict the lecture's two main topics.

B Watch or listen to Part 1 of the lecture. Follow along as you listen, using the handouts. Notice the additional notes a student added to each handout. Write a question mark next to anything you do not understand.

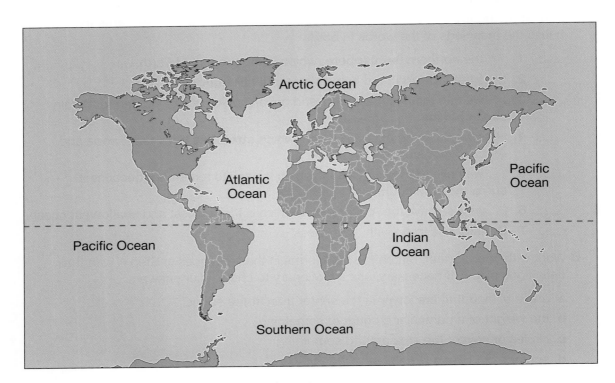

2 hemispheres: northern, top; southern, bottom
61% N. hem. ocean
80% S. hem. ocean
∴ Earth's surface = 71% ocean, 29% land

4 main basins: Atlantic – b/t Eur and Africa + Americas
     Pacific – largest + deepest; b/t Americas + Asia
     Indian – around India
     Arctic – in northern regions, smallest + shallowest
+ Southern – surrounds Ant.
All ocns connected, all water mix ⟶ 1 world ocn
Ocn is deep – average 4,200 meters
Ocn has layers b/c seaH₂0 has different densities

C Ask a partner any questions you have about the handout or the information you heard in the first part of the lecture.

1 Guessing vocabulary from context Ⓥ

A The following items contain important vocabulary from Part 2 of the lecture. Work with a partner. Using the context and your knowledge of related words, take turns trying to guess the meanings of the words in **bold**.

_____ **1.** The surface layer is sometimes called the "sunlit zone." Its warmth and light **permeate** the surface layer, making it an ideal place for many forms of life.

_____ **2.** Most of the ocean's fish and other **marine** life are near the surface layer . . .

_____ **3.** . . . they can find a lot of **algae** and other plants to eat.

_____ **4.** . . . the surface layer is **relatively** warm, with an average temperature of 17 degrees Celsius.

_____ **5.** . . . there is no sunlight here at all, so the water is **pitch black**.

_____ **6.** As a result, this layer is sometimes called the "**midnight** zone."

_____ **7.** The animals that live here have to **adapt** to be able to live in this cold and dark environment.

_____ **8.** It's the last **unexplored** region on Earth.

B Work with your partner. Match the bold terms in the sentences in Step A with their definitions below. If necessary, use a dictionary to check your answers.

a. not yet visited or studied

b. completely dark

c. spread throughout

d. relating to the sea

e. change to be able to live in a particular environment

f. the middle of the night

g. in comparison with other things

h. simple plants that live in or near water

2 Using handouts to help you take notes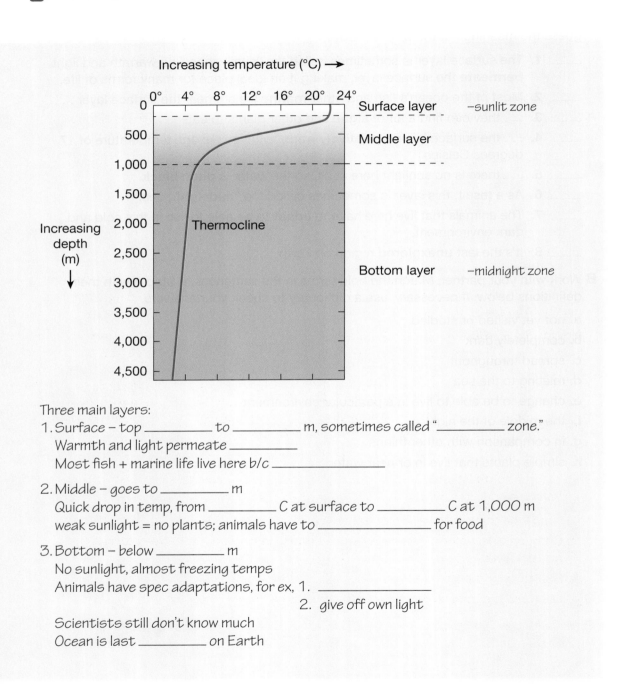

🔊 **A** Look at the handout below. As you listen to the second part of the lecture, fill in the
📹   missing information.

Increasing temperature (°C) →

0°   4°   8°   12° 16° 20° 24°

Surface layer   –sunlit zone

Middle layer

Thermocline

Bottom layer   –midnight zone

Increasing depth (m) ↓

Three main layers:

1. Surface – top _____ to _____ m, sometimes called "_____ zone."
   Warmth and light permeate _____
   Most fish + marine life live here b/c _____

2. Middle – goes to _____ m
   Quick drop in temp, from _____ C at surface to _____ C at 1,000 m
   weak sunlight = no plants; animals have to _____ for food

3. Bottom – below _____ m
   No sunlight, almost freezing temps
   Animals have spec adaptations, for ex, 1. _____
                                             2. give off own light

   Scientists still don't know much
   Ocean is last _____ on Earth

B Compare notes with a partner.

3 Focusing on the conclusion Ⓝ Ⓛ Ⓢ

> When the lecturer seems ready to conclude the lecture, do not stop paying attention. A lecturer will often summarize or emphasize the main points during the conclusion. This is a good opportunity to check your notes. You will know that a lecturer is about to conclude when you hear expressions like the following:
>
> | | | | |
> |---|---|---|---|
> | *In conclusion* | *In short* | *To review* | *Let me summarize* |
> | *In closing* | *Let's review* | *To summarize* | *Let me conclude by saying* |

A Watch or listen to the conclusion of the lecture. As Dr. Jackson reviews the main topics, check your notes to make sure you have written down information about each topic.

B Compare your notes with a partner.

AFTER THE LECTURE

Making test questions from your notes Ⓝ Ⓥ

> Making questions from your lecture notes is a good way to review and prepare for a test. In addition to the "Five Ws" (*who*, *what*, *where*, *when*, *why*), you can use the following words.
>
> | **Name:** | **Define:** | **Describe:** | **Explain:** | **Compare:** |
> |---|---|---|---|---|
> | Say what something is called | Give the meaning of something | Tell about the appearance, nature, or character of something | Give details to make something clear or to help someone understand something | Tell how something is similar to or different from something else |

A The following questions were written by a student in Dr. Jackson's class. Work with a partner and use your lecture notes to answer each question.

1. Name the three main layers of the ocean.
2. Compare the water temperature in the surface layer with the temperature in the bottom layer.
3. Explain why the bottom layer is sometimes called the "midnight zone."
4. Describe the marine life you would find at each level.

B Make four or five questions from your notes. Use a different question word for each question.

C Take turns asking and answering questions with your partner.

Unit 2 Academic Vocabulary Review

This section reviews the vocabulary from Chapters 3 and 4. Some of the words that you needed to learn to understand the content of this unit are specific to its topics. Other words are more general. They appear across different academic fields and are extremely useful for all students to know. For a complete list of all the Academic Word List words in this book, see the Appendix on page 180.

A Read the sentences and fill in the blanks with a form of the word.

1. **access (n), accessible (adj):**

   Having _____ to clean water is important for the health of any community.

2. **adapt (v), adaptation (n):**

   Many animals have been able to _____ to their surroundings.

3. **consequence (n), consequently (adv):**

   Without rain, rivers can dry up, and _____ animals sometimes have to go to other places to find water or food.

4. **constant (adj), constantly (adv):**

   Earth's water is _____ changing in form.

5. **cooperate (v), cooperation (n):**

   All countries should _____ to make sure we have clean water for everyone.

6. **environment (n), environmental (adj):**

   Bottled water is bad for the _____.

7. **location (n), located (adj):**

   A large amount of the world's freshwater is _____ in Canada.

8. **region (n), regional (adj):**

   The bottom of the ocean is the last unexplored _____ on Earth.

9. **transport (v), transportation (n):**

   Water is not only for drinking; it has also been used for _____ for centuries.

10. **resource (n), resourceful (adj):**

    We should all learn to look at water as a precious natural _____ that shouldn't be wasted.

B Use the academic vocabulary from Step A above to answer the following questions in pairs or as a class.

The Water We Drink

1. Why is access to clean drinking water important?
2. Why is bottled water a problem?
3. What can happen if people drink water that isn't clean?

Our Freshwater Supply

4. How does freshwater sometimes get polluted?
5. Why is freshwater called our most important natural resource?
6. What is the biggest problem facing the freshwater supply on Earth?

Ocean Adventures

7. What are some popular activities people do in the ocean?
8. Why don't surfers like to surf on days that are very windy?
9. What kinds of dangers can divers sometimes face?

One World Ocean

10. What does the term "one world ocean" mean?
11. What causes different layers of the ocean to be heavier, or denser, than others?
12. Why are animals at the bottom of the ocean different from those that live near the top of the ocean?

Oral Presentation

As a student, you will often participate in group presentations. Preparing and giving a group presentation helps you develop collaboration and leadership skills. Group presentations have to be carefully structured so that all members have an opportunity to speak. You should practice your presentation with your group members so that you can transition smoothly from one speaker to the next.

BEFORE THE PRESENTATION

1 Collect data

For this presentation, you will collect data about daily water usage. You will share the results with your group members. Then the group will make a usage report.

A Make a water usage journal like the one below. For one day, write down every activity you do that requires water. If possible, include the approximate amount of water you use.

	TASK	NOTES
Morning	flushed toilet brushed teeth washed face drank coffee (2 cups)	I usually leave the water on while I'm brushing my teeth. I could use less water if I turned off the tap.
Afternoon		
Evening		

B Share your water usage journal with your group members. Create a water usage report like the one below. Include every activity from each member's journal and the total number of times it occurred in one day.

GROUP DAILY WATER USAGE REPORT	
ACTIVITY	TOTAL GROUP USAGE
Flushing toilet	20 flushes
Showering	5 showers
Brushing teeth	8 times
Drinking water	about 4 liters
Washing hands	15 times
Giving water to pet	about 1 liter

2 Organize your presentation

A Assign different sections of the presentation to each member of the group. Make sure each member speaks for approximately the same amount of time.

Here is one suggestion for dividing the presentation:

Speaker 1: Introduce the topic and each member of the group.

Speaker 2: Present the group's water usage report.

Speaker 3: Explain the group's analysis of the water usage report (the most common activities, the least common activities, surprising results, etc.).

Speaker 4: Present the group's ideas for two or three ways we can use less water.

Speaker 5: Conclude the presentation (summarize the findings, comment on the project, give a final message to the class).

Speaker 1: Ask the audience if they have any questions or comments.

NOTE: You do not have to organize your presentation exactly this way. Just make sure each member knows his/her assigned part and the order of speakers.

B Prepare a visual aid for your group's presentation. This could be a poster, drawings, or pictures, or a graphic representation of your water usage results. Make your visual aid large enough to be seen by all members of your class. Remember that an effective visual aid helps communicate information clearly to your audience.

1 Use signal words and phrases

In this unit, you practiced listening for signal words and phrases to help you understand a lecture. When you give a presentation, you should use signal words and phrases to help your audience understand the organization and content of your speech.

Here are some signal words and phrases that you can use.

First / Second / Third   For example / For instance

Now / Next   On the other hand / In contrast / However

In addition / Furthermore   Finally / In conclusion

You may also want to review the signal words and phrases that you read about on pages 11, 30, 71, and 77.

2 Transition to other speakers

When you give a group presentation, transitioning from one speaker to the next will help your audience follow your speech. Here are some expressions you can use to transition between speakers.

First I will present our group's water usage report. After that, _____ will explain our analysis of the findings.

Thank you, _____ . Now that you've heard our group's water usage report, I would like to share our group's opinions about our findings.

As _____ just explained to you, we use a lot of water every day. Next I would like to tell you some ideas our group has for using less water.

Now I'd like to introduce _____ , who will conclude our presentation.

Respond to questions and comments

At the end of your presentation, allow at least five minutes for audience questions. You can improve your audience's understanding of your speech if you can respond to their questions and clarify any information they may have missed. Take turns in your group so that each member has a chance to answer a question.

When it is your turn to be an audience member, listen carefully to the other groups' presentations. Then ask the presenters questions or make a comment. Below are some expressions you can use.

QUESTIONS/COMMENTS	RESPONSES
Could you explain more about . . . ?	Sure, let me give you more details about that.
I didn't understand the part about . . .	Let me explain that again.
Can you give me an example of . . . ?	A good example is . . .
What did you mean when you said . . . ?	That's a good question. What I meant was . . .
I agree (disagree) with what you said about . . .	Thank you for your comment.

Unit 3
The Air Around Us

This unit explores Earth's atmosphere, or the air that surrounds us. In Chapter 5, you are going to listen to people talk about air quality. You will learn about some things that are in the air around you and where those things come from. Chapter 6 focuses on two important topics related to our atmosphere: weather and climate. You will hear an interview with a student majoring in meteorology (weather science) and stories from people who have experienced severe weather. The lecture is about the issue of global warming and its effects on our planet.

Contents

In Unit 3, you will listen to and speak about the following topics.

Skills

In Unit 3, you will practice the following skills.

L Listening Skills	**S** Speaking Skills
Listening for background noise Listening for specific information Answering multiple-choice questions Listening for opinions Listening for numerical information Listening for cause and effect	Examining a map Sharing your experience Conducting an experiment Predicting the content Applying what you have learned Personalizing the topic Understanding humor about the topic Thinking critically about the topic
V Vocabulary Skills	**N** Note Taking Skills
Reading and thinking about the topic Building background knowledge and vocabulary Understanding scientific symbols Examining vocabulary in context Identifying key vocabulary in the lecture Guessing vocabulary from context	Organizing your notes in an outline Organizing your notes in a chart Copying a lecturer's illustrations

Learning Outcomes

Prepare and **deliver** an oral presentation about global warming with a partner

Chapter 5
Earth's Atmosphere

Look at the photographs and answer the questions with a partner.

1. What do these photographs show? Use adjectives to describe the air in both photos.

2. Why is air quality important? What are the effects of air pollution? Think about plants and animals as well as humans.

1 Getting Started

In this section, you are going to think about how and why air quality varies in different parts of the world. You will hear people describing the air quality in different places.

1 Reading and thinking about the topic Ⓥ Ⓢ

A Read the following passage.

The air on Earth is made up of more than 10 different gases, including nitrogen, oxygen, and carbon dioxide. Although air everywhere is made up of the same gases, air quality can vary from place to place. For example, the air in a crowded, industrial city feels and smells different from the air at a beach. The air at the top of a mountain does not feel the same as the air in a rain forest or in a desert.

Many factors affect air quality. One is humidity, or how much water is in the air. Another is the amount of particulates, which are small pieces of dirt, dust, and other matter. Finally, air pressure (how strongly the air presses around us on Earth's surface) also affects air quality.

B Answer the following questions according to the information in the passage. Share your answers with a partner.

1. Is the air everywhere on Earth the same? Explain.

2. What are three factors that affect air quality? Define each factor.

C Read the following questions and share your answers with a partner.

1. Describe the air in the place where you live now. Does it feel clean or dirty? Humid or dry? Do you feel comfortable breathing the air where you live?

2. Have you ever been to a big city, a beach, a mountain, a rain forest, or a desert? If so, describe how the air smells and feels in those places.

2 Listening for background noise ⓛ ⓥ ⓢ

> When you listen, you should focus on what people are saying. But sometimes you can get useful information by listening to background noise as well.

A Look at the people in the pictures below. Work with a partner. Describe what the people in the photos are doing, how they are feeling, and why. Use the following gerunds.

Sneezing: what you do when something irritates your nose

Coughing: what you do when something irritates your lungs or throat

Sweating: what you do when you are hot

Gasping: what you do when you have trouble breathing

a.

b.

c.

d.

B Now listen to the people and decide where they are. Write a, b, c, or d.

____ in the countryside

____ at the top of a mountain

____ in a city

____ in a rain forest

C Now listen again as the people say why they are having problems. Match the person with what is causing his or her problem. Write a, b, c, or d.

____ The air is thin.

____ There's a lot of pollen in the air.

____ It is very hot and humid.

____ The air is dirty.

D Work with a partner. Take turns describing the person in each picture using the language below.

This person is	in the countryside	and is	sneezing	because	there's pollen in the air.
	in a city		coughing		it's dirty.
	in a rain forest		sweating		it is very humid.
	at the top of a mountain		gasping		the air is thin.

2 Real-Life Voices

In this section, you are going to hear four people talk about some factors that influence air quality: particulates, smog, humidity, and dryness. They will also describe how these factors affect people.

BEFORE THE INTERVIEWS

1 Building background knowledge and vocabulary

> When people talk about scientific topics, they often use technical vocabulary that is specific to the topic. If you learn some of these words before listening to a lecture or conversation, it will help your comprehension.

A Each picture below shows a source of particulates, very small pieces of matter that float around in the air. Most particulate matter is so small that we cannot see it. Particulates come from both natural and human-made sources. Write the number of the correct picture next to each source.

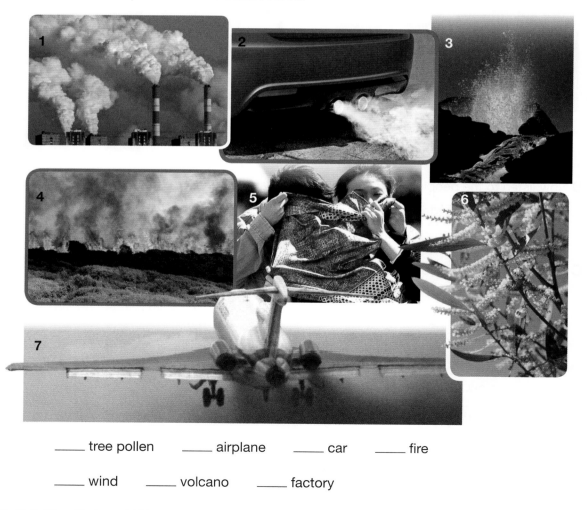

_____ tree pollen   _____ airplane   _____ car   _____ fire

_____ wind   _____ volcano   _____ factory

B Fill in the chart using the words in Step A.

Sources of particulate matter	
Natural sources	Human-made sources

C Add one more source of particulate matter to each column of the chart in Step B. Compare your answers with a partner.

2 Examining a map Ⓢ

A Look at the map below and answer the questions.

   1. What generalizations or patterns can you see in humidity and dryness?

   2. Which continent is the driest? Explain your answer.

   3. What is the climate like in your part of the world?

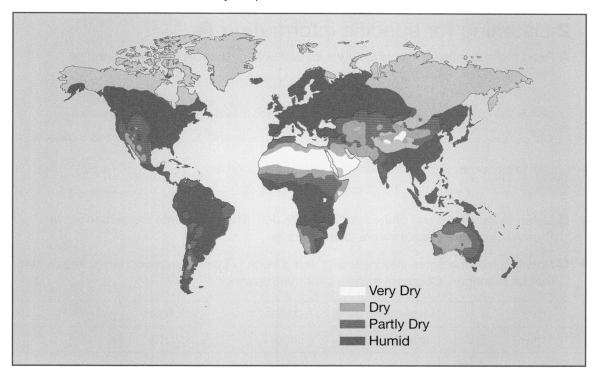

Very Dry
Dry
Partly Dry
Humid

B Locate the area where you live on the map. Discuss the questions below with a partner.

   1. How does the weather change from season to season in the area where you live?

   2. Think about how you feel when the air is very dry or very humid. Does it affect your breathing? Your skin? Your body temperature? In what other ways does it affect you?

   3. Do you prefer living in a dry area or a humid area? Why?

1 Examining vocabulary in context Ⓥ

The words in **bold** are given in the context in which you will hear them in the interview. Definitions follow.

> There are a lot of **pollutants** in the air: *something that harms the water, air, land, or other resources or that makes them unusable*

> The most common human-made pollutants that you see come from burning **fuels**: *oil, natural gas, or coal*

> . . . tiny pieces of matter that are small enough to **float** in the air: *move in the air without falling to the ground*

> . . . you might see a black or gray **coating** on cars: *a layer of something that covers a surface*

> . . . it can cause **damage** to our **lungs**: *physical harm / the organs in the body used for breathing*

> . . . a wildfire that starts naturally from **lightning**: *a flash in the sky caused by an electrical discharge, usually during a thunderstorm*

2 Listening for specific information Ⓛ

A Read the summary of the interview with Jeff below. Think about what kinds of information might go in the blanks.

> Jeff is the director of an environmental organization. He is always thinking about
>
> _____ _____ and its effects on _____ and _____ . In this interview,
>
> Jeff talks about _____ that affect air quality, such as _____ in the air.

🔊 **B** Listen to the beginning of the interview with Jeff. Then complete the sentences in Step A. Compare your answers with a partner.

🔊 **C** Now listen to the entire interview with Jeff. Check (✓) the sources of particulate matter that he mentions. Compare answers with your partner.

cars	airplanes	factories	volcanoes
trees	windstorms	wildfire	cigarette smoke

INTERVIEW 2 Air Quality

1 Examining vocabulary in context Ⓥ

The words in **bold** are given in the context in which you will hear them in the interview. Definitions follow.

> It looks **hazy**: *not clear*
>
> . . . it's like **fog**, but it's brown like smoke: *clouds in the air close to the ground that make it difficult to see*
>
> During the weather report, they always include a **smog level advisory**: *news reports advising people about the current air quality*
>
> . . . when we went to **P.E.**: *physical education; a class in which students exercise and play sports*

2 Listening for specific information Ⓛ Ⓢ

🔊 **A** Look at the list of effects that poor air quality can have on people and the environment. Listen to Shari talk about living in a city with poor air quality and complete the sentences.

Effects of poor air quality

1. Shari can't see the _____ near her home.
2. The color of the air is _____ .
3. Shari gets bad _____ .
4. It is difficult for Shari to _____ .
5. At school, children can't _____ outside.

🔊 **B** Listen again to this part of the interview with Shari and complete the sentences.

1. Smog comes from the words _____ and _____ mixed together . . .
2. Anytime it's over three or four, they _____ people to be careful.

C Compare your answers to Steps A and B with a partner.

Chapter 5 *Earth's Atmosphere* **91**

1 Examining vocabulary in context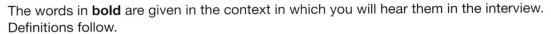

The words in **bold** are given in the context in which you will hear them in the interview. Definitions follow.

I know that you're a very **athletic** person: *good at sports or playing sports frequently*

You need to get rid of some of that heat by **sweating**: *to lose moisture through the skin*

. . . the sweat can **evaporate** and cool your skin: *change from a liquid to a gas; disappear*

So when it's humid, it's harder to **cool your body down**: *return to a normal temperature after being hot*

. . . "This is **crazy**, let's get out of here!": *not normal, unusual*

Did living in the desert affect you **physically**: *in your body*

. . . a gallon of **sports drinks** a day: *beverages that help resupply the body with fluids*

2 Answering multiple-choice questions ⓛ ⓢ

A Read the following questions before you listen to the interview. Circle the answer that you think is correct.

1. According to Kelley, the most important factor for athletes is the _____ .
   a. temperature of the air   **b.** humidity of the air

2. Sweating helps take the _____ out of our bodies.
   a. heat   **b.** fat

3. When the air is humid, it is harder for the body to _____ .
   a. cool down   **b.** warm up

4. When the air is humid, you may feel more _____ than usual.
   a. tired   **b.** hungry

5. While living in the desert, Michael experienced a _____ .
   a. dust storm   **b.** thunderstorm

6. In the desert, Michael noticed that he _____ a lot more than usual.
   a. slept   **b.** drank

7. Some physical effects of dry air are _____ .
   a. headaches and a sore throat   **b.** dry lips and skin

8. Michael thinks it is not a good idea to exercise in the desert because _____ .
   a. the hot, dry air almost hurts your lungs   **b.** there is a lot of particulate matter in the air

B Listen to the interview with Kelley and Michael. Check your answers to the questions in Step A.

C Share your answers with a partner.

AFTER THE INTERVIEWS

Sharing your experience Ⓢ

In a small group, discuss places you have been where the air has been very clean, very polluted, very humid, or very dry. Talk about how the air made you feel in each of those places. Did you notice any other effects? Fill in the chart with notes from the group discussion.

Air quality	Places	Effects
Clean air		
Polluted air		
Humid air		
Dry air		

3 In Your Own Voice

In this section, you are going to conduct an experiment to measure the particulate matter in the air. You will also compare the air quality at two different locations. Finally, you will present your research findings to the class.

Conducting an experiment

> When you read scientific information, sometimes it is possible to conduct, or do, your own experiment to confirm it. This will help you understand the information better.

Materials needed

| Two index cards (or other stiff paper) | Clear packing tape | String | Scissors | Optional: magnifying glass or microscope |

Procedure

1. Cut a 3 x 5 cm rectangle out of the center of one index card. Place a large piece of clear tape over the hole on one side of the card. Be careful to keep the sticky side of the tape over the hole clean.

Sticky

2. Using the string, hang your card outside. Choose a place where the card will not be touched by people or anything else for at least one day. This is your first location.

3. Take notes on the following:
   - Approximately how high did you hang your card?
   - How windy is it?
   - What is the weather like (for example, the temperature, the humidity, etc.)?

4. Repeat Steps 1 through 3 with the second index card. This time, hang the card at your second location.

5. Wait at least 24 hours. Collect both cards and look at the particulate matter stuck to the tape. If possible, study the particulate matter with a magnifying glass or microscope. Then record answers to the following questions.

- Count the number of particles in the 3 x 5 cm rectangle. Are all the particles the same, or are there different types of particles?
- Can you identify any of them?
- What do you think the sources of the particulate matter are?
- Which location had more particulate matter in the air? Are there any other differences in the particulate matter at the two locations?
- Did the weather or any other factors influence the results of your experiment?

Presenting your results

Prepare a short oral report about your experiment. Use the note cards below to help you. Remember to practice your report a few times before presenting it in front of the class.

Good morning. / Good afternoon.
I conducted an experiment to investigate air quality in two locations. One location was _____ . The second location was _____ .
In the first location, I hung my card . . . (describe location, height, and duration). In the second location, I hung my card . . .

Here are the results of my experiment. At the first location, I found . . .
At the second location, I found . . .
I think some of the sources of the particulate matter are . . .
The amount of particulate matter in the air is more / less than I expected.
Something I learned from conducting this experiment is . . .

4 Academic Listening and Note Taking

In this section, you are going to hear and take notes on a two-part lecture, "What Is in the Air Out There?" by Ken Needham, an Earth science teacher. Mr. Needham will discuss three things that can be found in the air: gases, water, and particulate matter.

BEFORE THE LECTURE

1 Predicting the content Ⓢ Ⓛ

A The answers to the questions below can be found in this chapter on the pages you have already read. Work with a partner and try to answer the questions without looking back. Then compare answers as a class.

1. How many gases are in air?
2. What are two important gases that can be found in air?
3. What word describes air when there is a lot of moisture in it?
4. What word describes air when there is not much moisture in it?
5. What is the name for solid matter that is floating in the air?
6. What word describes air when it has a lot of solid matter in it?
7. What are two natural sources of the solid matter?
8. What are two human-made sources of the solid matter?
9. What physical problems do people suffer from when there is a lot of solid matter in the air?

B In the lecture, Mr. Needham talks about the level of humidity in the air. Which level do you think is the most comfortable for most people? Put a check (✓) next to your prediction.

_____ 10 percent   _____ 50 percent   _____ 80 percent

C In the lecture, Mr. Needham also talks about how moisture gets into the air. What do you think are some major sources of humidity? Write your answer below.

_____

_____

2 Identifying key vocabulary in the lecture ⓥ ⓝ ⓛ

When a lecturer defines a word, it usually means that it is an important word to learn and remember. Notice when a lecturer gives a definition and write the word and definition in your notes. This is also a good technique for learning new vocabulary.

Here are some examples of phrases a lecturer may use to define key vocabulary.
X can be defined as . . .   *. . . X; in other words, . . .*   *. . . This is called X.*
. . . X, that is, . . .   *. . . X, or . . .*   *. . . This is known as X.*

A Watch or listen to several excerpts from the lecture. As you hear the words or phrases below, match them to their definitions.

_____ **1.** humidity level
_____ **2.** particulate matter
_____ **3.** pollen
_____ **4.** pollution

a. substances in the air that shouldn't be there; too much of certain substances that make the air dirty
b. tiny pieces of solid matter floating in the air
c. a powder made by flowers
d. the amount of water vapor in the air

B Watch or listen again. Match the words or phrases with the language in the definitions you hear.

1. humidity level
2. particulate matter
3. pollen
4. pollution

a. The term X is defined as . . .
b. . . . X, or . . .
c. . . . and this is what we know as X.
d. . . . in other words, X . . .

C Compare answers with a partner.

1 Guessing vocabulary from context Ⓥ

A The following items are from Part 1 of the lecture. Work with a partner. Using the context and your knowledge of related words, take turns trying to guess the meanings of the words in **bold**.

_____ **1.** . . . air actually **contains** many different things.

_____ **2.** . . . the air around you is **composed of** a lot of different gases.

_____ **3.** . . . your clothes will probably feel **sticky** . . .

_____ **4.** The most obvious **source** is rain, snow, and other forms of liquid or solid water . . .

B Work with your partner. Match the terms in bold in the sentences in Step A with their definitions below. If necessary, use a dictionary to check your answers.

a. origin

b. damp, wet; like glue

c. is made of

d. has; includes

2 Organizing your notes in an outline Ⓝ Ⓛ

You may not have enough time to organize your notes in an outline while you are actually listening to a lecture, but do try to do it as soon as possible afterward. Putting your notes in an outline or other organized format while they are still fresh in your mind will help you remember what you learned.

A Look at the partial outline of Part 1 of the lecture on the next page. Think about the kinds of information you might need to complete the outline.

The Air We Breathe

I. Gases
    A. Nitrogen makes up _____ %
    B. _____ makes up 21%
    C. Also _____ other gases

II. Water
    A. Vapor is the form of most water in the air
    B. Amount of water in air is called _____
        1. _____ %
            a. high level: lots of water in air
            b. probably feel _____
        2. 50%
            a. _____
            b. most people feel _____
        3. _____ %
            a. _____ + other dry places
            b. not much water in air
    C. Sources of water
        1. most obvious – liquids or solids that fall from the clouds,
          e.g., _____ , _____
        2. _____ + _____
        3. _____ + _____
        4. _____

B Watch or listen to Part 1 of the lecture. As you listen, fill in the missing information in the outline in Step A. Pay attention to key vocabulary words that are defined in the lecture.

C Compare outlines with a partner.

D Check your answers to Steps B and C on page 96. Were they correct?

1 Guessing vocabulary from context Ⓥ

A The following items are from Part 2 of the lecture. Work with a partner. Using the context and your knowledge of related words, take turns trying to guess the meanings of the words in **bold**.

_____ **1.** Have you ever thought about the idea of **solids** in the air?

_____ **2.** When a volcano erupts, it shoots smoke and **ash** into the air.

_____ **3.** When the ocean waves **crash** against the shore . . .

_____ **4.** Flowers, trees, plants – they **release** pollen . . .

_____ **5.** That might be **pollen** in the air entering your nose.

_____ **6.** Dirt and dust . . . fly into our eyes and make them red and **itchy**.

_____ **7.** . . . there are some **substances** in the air that shouldn't be there . . .

_____ **8.** The activity that creates the most pollution is the burning of coal and other **fossil fuels**.

B Work with your partner. Match the terms in **bold** in the sentences in Step A with their definitions below. If necessary, use a dictionary to check your answers.

a. to hit hard against something

b. coal, oil, natural gas, or other energy sources that come from things that lived long ago

c. uncomfortable; making you want to rub or scratch your body with your fingers

d. powder that erupts from a volcano in a gas cloud

e. not liquids or gases; substances that keep their shape

f. matter or material that makes up something

g. a fine powder in a seed plant

h. to let go of something

2 Organizing your notes in a chart Ⓝ Ⓥ

Using a chart is a good way to organize your notes if a lecturer gives a lot of examples and supporting details. You can also use charts to review before a test.

A Look at the chart made from notes on Part 2 of the lecture. Think about the kind of information you might need to complete the chart.

Types of particulate matter			
Natural		Human-made	
Source	**Particles**	**Action**	**Result**
	smoke, ash		more particulate matter added to air
forest fire		cut down trees and take water	
ocean waves			pollution added to air
	pollen, natural matter		
environment			

🔊 **B** Watch or listen to Part 2 of the lecture. As you listen, fill in the missing information in the chart.

C Compare your chart with a partner.

Applying what you have learned Ⓢ Ⓥ

Work in a small group. Look at these pictures and discuss what the quality of the air might be like in each place. Take notes. Be prepared to explain your answers using details and vocabulary from the chapter.

Chapter 6
Weather and Climate

1 Getting Started

In this section, you are going to learn the difference between weather and climate.
You will also hear some weather reports and practice using weather symbols.

1 Reading and thinking about the topic Ⓥ Ⓢ

A Read the following passage.

Weather is the condition of the atmosphere at a certain time and place. When you look out the window, you can check the weather outside: Is it warm and sunny, windy and rainy, or cold and snowy? Nearly all weather forms in the troposphere, the layer of the atmosphere closest to Earth's surface. Weather can change quickly from one day to the next, or even within the same day.

In contrast, climate changes very slowly. Climate is the usual weather in an area over many years. Scientists look at weather over a period of 20 or more years to find weather patterns. Then, based on the patterns, they can describe the area's climate as dry, tropical, mild, variable, or polar.

B Answer the following questions according to the information in the passage.

1. Define the following words: *weather*, *climate*, *troposphere*.
2. If you say, "I live in a dry area," are you talking about the weather or the climate? Explain.
3. Name five different types of climates.

C Read the following questions and share your answers with a partner.

1. Describe the climate in the place where you grew up. What is the weather usually like at this time of year?
2. What is your favorite kind of weather? Why?

2 Understanding scientific symbols ⓥ

People often use symbols to represent scientific concepts. As you study science, you will learn to understand and use symbols.

A Meteorologists (scientists who study the weather) use symbols to describe the weather. Look at this chart of weather symbols.

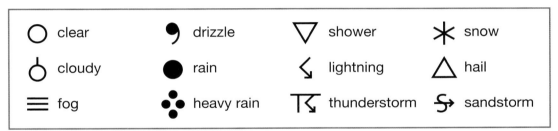

○ clear	❦ drizzle	▽ shower	✳ snow
♀ cloudy	● rain	⟨ lightning	△ hail
≡ fog	⣿ heavy rain	Ⱦ thunderstorm	⇝ sandstorm

B Now use the chart to write a word or phrase for each type of weather represented.

1. ⬇ _____

2. ✳✳✳ _____

3. ≡● _____

4. △Ⱦ _____

3 Listening for specific information 🅛

A Read the four weather reports. Think about what kinds of information might go in the blanks.

1. The sky is _____ and there are no _____ .
   Temperatures are _____ here.

2. The sky is _____ . The _____ is strong. In about an hour, a _____ will start.

3. The temperature is getting _____ . Soon the _____ will change to _____ .

4. The heavy _____ has ended, but we're still going to have a lot of _____ today.

🔊 **B** Now listen to the weather reports and use the words below to fill in the missing information in Step A. One of the words will be used twice.

wind	rain	warm	clouds
clear	cloudy	snow	colder
thunderstorm	fog		

C Which symbols would meteorologists use to describe the current conditions for each weather report in Step A? Fill in each box with the correct symbols.

1.

2.

3.

4.

2 Real-Life Voices

In this section, you are going to hear a student talk about her major, meteorology.

BEFORE THE INTERVIEWS

Personalizing the topic Ⓢ Ⓥ

A Work in a small group. Read the weather events and their definitions below.

hurricane: a storm with heavy rain and very strong winds that begins over the ocean	**blizzard:** a winter storm with a lot of snow and strong winds	**flood:** a large amount of water that covers a land area that is usually dry	**heat wave:** a period of unusually hot weather

B In your group, discuss whether anyone has experienced the weather events in Step A. If someone answers Yes, write his or her name in the chart below.

Have you ever experienced a . . .

hurricane	blizzard	flood	heat wave

C Choose one weather event that you have experienced from the chart and describe it to your group. Give the details, including answers to the following questions:

- When did it happen?
- How did you feel?
- What did you see?
- What were the effects?

1 Examining vocabulary in context ⓥ

Here are some words and phrases from the interview with Sara printed in **bold** and given in the context in which you will hear them. They are followed by definitions.

> . . . right now I'm a **graduate student**: *someone studying for a degree after completing a four-year college degree*
>
> It is a way of **describing** and trying to understand what happens: *telling what something is, what it looks like, etc.*
>
> I guess he **influenced** me: *affected someone or something*
>
> I've always had a **fascination** with the sky: *a strong interest*
>
> When I was young, I would **stare at** the sky: *to look at for a long time, usually with great concentration*
>
> Earth is like a big **aquarium**: *a clear glass container for fish to live in*

2 Listening for specific information ⓛ ⓝ

A Read the profile of Sara below. Think about what kinds of information might go in the blanks.

> *Name:* Sara _____
>
> *Country of origin:* _____
>
> *Major:* _____
>
> *Meteorology is the study of* _____.
>
> *She decided to study meteorology because:*
>
> *1.* _____
>
> *2.* _____

🔊 **B** Now listen to the interview with Sara. Listen for the information that you need to complete the blanks in Step A and write it in the blanks.

🔊 **C** A *simile* is a way of describing something by comparing it to something else. Similes use the word *like*. Listen to the last part of the interview again. What similes does Sara use?

Earth is like _____ . . .

. . . we're just like _____ . . .

. . . our atmosphere is just like _____ .

1 Examining vocabulary in context Ⓥ

Here are some words and phrases from the interview with Dorothy, Yukiya, and Evylynn printed in **bold** and given in the context in which you will hear them. They are followed by definitions.

Dorothy

It really was a **freak** storm: *very unusual*

Generally we don't get much snow in New York in October: *as a rule; usually; typically*

And then, when the tree branches broke, they fell onto the **power lines**: *large wires that carry electricity*

Yukiya

. . . I saw all this water **pouring** into the parking lot: *moving quickly and in large amounts*

I actually saw one car **floating**: *moving on the surface of water*

And all around me there was water and **mud**: *wet, soft earth, like after it rains*

I was **soaking wet**: *completely wet*

Evylynn

When I was 16 years old, a hurricane **struck** my hometown: *hit*

It was a **Category 4** hurricane: *the strength of a powerful hurricane (Category 1 is the weakest and Category 5 is the strongest)*

Houses right across the street from me were **torn apart**: *broken into pieces*

Of course I was worried about the families in the houses that were **destroyed**: *completely broken; no longer able to be used*

2 Predicting the content Ⓛ Ⓢ

A Review the four kinds of severe weather you studied in "Before the Interviews" on page 105. Now review the information in the vocabulary presentation above. Can you predict which kind of severe weather each interviewee experienced? Write your guesses below.

Dorothy was in a _____ .	**Yukiya** got caught in a _____ .	**Evylynn** experienced a _____ .

B Now listen to excerpts from the interview. Check your guesses in Step A.

C Read each statement below. Guess if it is spoken by Dorothy, Yukiya, or Evylynn.

_____ **1.** . . . trees and lampposts were flying everywhere.

_____ **2.** Once you experience something like that, you remember it for the rest of your life.

_____ **3.** Houses right across the street from me were torn apart.

_____ **4.** I actually saw one car floating!

_____ **5.** . . . the weight of the snow brought down a lot of tree branches.

_____ **6.** I was like, "This is definitely going to be on the news!"

_____ **7.** . . . it was falling very fast, and by Friday morning we had about two feet of it.

D Now listen to the whole interview. Write _D_ (Dorothy), _Y_ (Yukiya), or _E_ (Evylynn) next to each statement in Step C.

E Compare your answers to Steps A and D with a partner.

3 Listening for opinions ⓛ

In this section, the interviewer is going to ask Sara, Dorothy, Yukiya, and Evylynn about global warming. She asks if they think global warming is affecting Earth's weather. Global warming is the increase in temperature of the Earth's atmosphere and oceans. Listen and circle each interviewee's answer. Take notes on the reasons they give for their opinions.

Do you think that global warming is affecting the weather on Earth?		Reasons for opinion
Sara	YES / NO / DON'T KNOW	
Dorothy	YES / NO / DON'T KNOW	
Yukiya	YES / NO / DON'T KNOW	
Evylynn	YES / NO / DON'T KNOW	

Understanding humor about the topic ⓢ

> If you can understand and appreciate humor, such as cartoons or jokes, about the topic of an interview, you have probably understood the main points.

Work in a small group. Look at the cartoons and discuss the following questions.

1. According to cartoons 1 and 2, what are some changes that global warming will cause to Earth?
2. What is the artist's message in cartoon 3? Do you agree with his opinion?
3. Do you think the cartoons are funny? Why or why not?
4. What do you think Sara, Dorothy, Yukiya, and Evylynn would think about the cartoons?

Barbecue Circa 2050

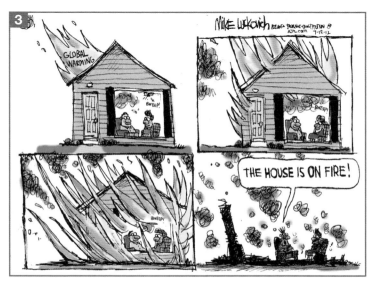

3 In Your Own Voice

In this section, you are going to brainstorm the good points and bad points about each of the seasons. Then you will participate in a group debate in which you support your favorite season.

Thinking critically about the topic Ⓢ

A Make a chart like the one below on a separate piece of paper. Working in a small group, discuss good points and bad points about each season. Write them in the chart.

	Good Points	Bad Points
Winter		
Spring		
Summer		
Fall		

B Choose the season you feel has the most good points, or the most important good points. Discuss why this season is "better" than the other seasons.

C Debate this issue with another small group that has chosen a different season. Take turns presenting the ideas in your chart and explaining why you chose the season you did. You can use some of the expressions below.

Presenting your ideas

There are many reasons we think . . . is the best season. First, . . .

Another reason we like . . . is that . . .

In addition, we think . . .

Responding to the other team

I'm afraid we don't agree with you, because . . .

I can see your point, but . . .

Yes, that may be true. However, . . .

4 Academic Listening and Note Taking

In this section, you are going to hear and take notes on a two-part lecture given by Dr. Fred Mackenzie, a researcher and author on climate change. In his lecture, "Global Warming," Dr. Mackenzie will first explain the greenhouse effect. Then he will discuss the effects of global warming.

1 Building background knowledge on the topic ⓥ ⓢ

In Dr. Mackenzie's lecture, you are going to hear about the greenhouse effect in Earth's atmosphere. Look at the picture of a real greenhouse below. If you understand how a real greenhouse works, you will understand the lecture better.

A Work with a partner. Look at the picture and discuss what you know about greenhouses.

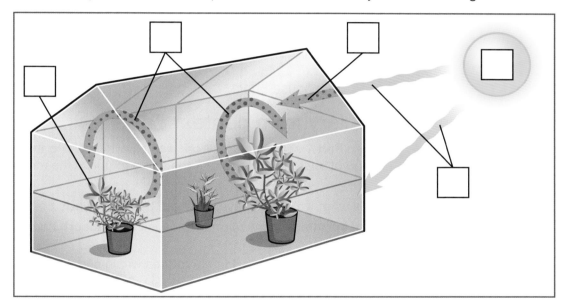

B Read the explanation of how a greenhouse works below. Work with your partner and label each box with the number of the correct sentence.

1. Energy comes from the sun.
2. Energy from the sun enters the greenhouse as light.
3. Inside the greenhouse, the light energy changes into heat energy.
4. The glass windows hold the heat energy inside the greenhouse.
5. The greenhouse stays warm and the plants grow.

C In the lecture, Dr. Mackenzie is going to explain the natural greenhouse effect of Earth's atmosphere. What do you think this is? Discuss your ideas with your partner.

2 Listening for numerical information

> Listening for numerical information is an important skill to practice because scientists often use this type of information to support their ideas. Scientific lectures often include years, percentages, temperatures, and other numbers representing scientific data.

A Read the sentences below. They give numerical information about Earth that you are going to hear in the lecture. Circle the phrase in parentheses that you think correctly completes each sentence.

1. The Earth is (*4.6 million years* / *4.6 billion years*) old.
2. (*Thirty-five percent* / *Seventy percent*) of the sun's energy passes through the atmosphere to Earth's surface.
3. Earth's temperature has increased (*1°C* / *5°C*) due to global warming.
4. (*Forty percent* / *Eighty percent*) of the world's energy comes from burning fossil fuels.

B Now watch or listen to the excerpts from the lecture. Check the phrases you circled in Step A and correct them if necessary. Then compare your answers with a partner.

LECTURE PART 1 The Greenhouse Effect

1 Guessing vocabulary from context

A The following items are from Part 1 of the lecture. Work with a partner. Using the context and your knowledge of related words, take turns trying to guess the meanings of the words in **bold**.

_____ 1. The atmosphere is what we call the layer of gases that **surrounds** the planet.

_____ 2. They [gases] make the atmosphere warmer, because they **absorb** heat from the sun.

_____ 3. This process helps to **maintain** global temperatures within certain limits.

_____ 4. What has happened in the past **century** or so is that human activities have added more greenhouse gases to the atmosphere.

_____ 5. While there has been some **debate**, I think people have realized that the increased greenhouse effect is causing the problem of global warming.

B Work with your partner. Match the vocabulary terms in Step A with their definitions below by writing the letter of each definition in the blank next to the sentence containing the correct term. Check your answers in a dictionary if necessary.

a. 100 years

b. take something in so that it becomes part of it

c. support; keep in good condition

d. occupies the space all around something

e. argument; disagreement; discussion

2 Copying a lecturer's illustrations Ⓝ Ⓛ Ⓢ

> When a lecturer draws an illustration on the board during a lecture, you should copy it into your notes. You can add extra information to the illustration as the lecturer speaks.

A Look at the illustration that Dr. Mackenzie talks about during Part 1 of his lecture. It explains the natural greenhouse effect on Earth. Think about what kinds of information you need to label the illustration.

B As you watch or listen to Part 1 of the lecture, number each of the events in the order that they are mentioned.

_____ **a.** Seventy percent passes through the atmosphere.

_____ **b.** Most of the warmth emitted by the Earth stays in our atmosphere.

_____ **c.** Half of that energy reaches the Earth's surface.

_____ **d.** Thirty percent of the sun's energy is reflected off the atmosphere.

_____ **e.** About ten percent of that energy is leaked back into space.

_____ **f.** Energy from the sun approaches the Earth.

_____ **g.** The Earth emits the sun's warmth back toward the atmosphere.

C Now write captions to go with the diagram in Step A. Use the answers in Step B. You can use abbreviations and shorten the sentences to save space.

1 Guessing vocabulary from context ⓥ

A The following items are from Part 2 of the lecture. Work with a partner. Using the context and your knowledge of related words, take turns trying to guess the meanings of the words in **bold**.

_____ 1. What are the **consequences** of this increase in Earth's temperature?

_____ 2. When ocean waters warm, they **expand**, or get bigger.

_____ 3. Already many countries around the world are experiencing more and longer periods of **drought** . . .

_____ 4. It's difficult to **predict** the future.

_____ 5. I think all of us, as **individuals**, must take action to solve this problem.

B Work with your partner. Match the vocabulary terms in Step A with their definitions below by writing the letter of each definition in the blank next to the sentence containing the correct term. Check your answers in a dictionary if necessary.

a. become bigger

b. a long period when there is not enough rain to grow crops or refill water supplies

c. each person

d. to guess something before it happens

e. results; effects

2 Listening for cause and effect Ⓛ Ⓝ Ⓢ

Lecturers often explain scientific concepts in terms of their causes and effects.
You should listen for words that signal cause-and-effect relationships so that you can
note this important information. Here are some examples of expressions that signal
cause and effect.

One cause of this is . . .	Consequently, . . .
This is due to . . .	As a result, . . . / . . . resulting in . . .
If [cause], then [effect]	One effect of this is . . .

A Read the excerpts from the lecture. Circle the cause in each excerpt. Underline
the effect(s).

1. "Some of this rise is due to the heating of the ocean surface. When ocean waters
warm, they expand, or get bigger, and so the sea level rises."

_____

2. "The melt water is entering the ocean and resulting in a rise in sea level."

_____

3. "Changes in the weather are another consequence of global warming."

_____

4. "Hurricanes develop over warm oceans, and so the rise in ocean temperatures may
cause more and perhaps stronger hurricanes."

_____

B Now rewrite the excerpts in Step A in note form on the blanks by shortening them to
key words only. Put the cause first, followed by an arrow and then the effect(s).
Use abbreviations, symbols, and telegraphic language where possible.

Example: "An increase of one degree centigrade may not seem like a lot, but it
actually causes many changes on our planet."

↑ one degree centigrade → many changes

C Watch or listen to Part 2 of the lecture. Take notes on a separate piece of paper.
Remember to listen for the expressions that signal cause and effect.

D Compare your notes with a partner.

Applying what you have learned Ⓢ

> Thinking about what you have learned in relation to current news or events – images in current magazines or in the TV news or trending online – is a good way to deepen your knowledge about a topic and to think of new questions.

A The melting of glaciers has been featured in print and news reports over the past several years, and it is the subject of many amateur online videos. Look at the images below. Work in a small group. Describe each image and explain how it might be connected to what you learned in this lecture.

Triftgletscher glacier, Switzerland, in 2002   The same location in 2003

B Discuss the following questions in small groups.

1. What questions do you have about global warming – its causes and its effects?

2. How can we encourage our government and business leaders to take the necessary steps to slow down or even reverse global warming?

3. What actions can we take as individuals to address global warming? How can scientists, politicians, artists, writers, businesspeople, farmers, educators, parents, and others help? How can investors help? How can we, as consumers, help?

Unit 3 Academic Vocabulary Review

This section reviews the vocabulary from Chapters 5 and 6. Some of the words that you needed to learn to understand the content of this unit are specific to its topics. Other words are more general. They appear across different academic fields and are extremely useful for all students to know. For a complete list of all the Academic Word List words in this book, see the Appendix on page 180.

A Read the sentences and fill in the blanks with the correct form of the word.

1. **debate (v), debatable (adj):**
   The causes of global warming are _____ .

2. **expand (v), expansion (n):**
   When we breathe in air, our lungs _____ .

3. **globe (n), global (adj):**
   The quality of the air we breathe is a _____ concern.

4. **individual (n), individually (adv):**
   There are things we can do _____ to protect the atmosphere.

5. **maintain (v), maintenance (n):**
   Our town has tried to _____ air quality by controlling manufacturing and agricultural activities.

6. **obvious (adj), obviously (adv):**
   _____ the atmosphere is affected by a variety of factors.

7. **consequence (n), consequentially (adv):**
   The greenhouse effect is a _____ of long-term pollution.

8. **release (v), released (adj):**
   Plants _____ pollen into the air.

9. **composed (adj), composition (n):**
   The air we breathe is _____ of gases.

10. **predict (v), prediction (n):**
    He has made a frightening _____ about the consequences of global warming.

11. **absorb (v), absorption (n):**
    Gases _____ heat from the sun.

12. **define (v), definition (n):**
    We can _____ vapor as water in gas form.

B Use the academic vocabulary from Step A above to answer the following questions in pairs or as a class.

Air Pollution

1. What are some causes of air pollution?
2. Can one single person do anything to reduce air pollution?
3. What sources of energy are the most and least harmful to air quality?

Breathing difficulties

4. What is pollen, and how does it affect people?
5. How do dryness and humidity affect some people's breathing?
6. What is a smog level advisory?

Different climates

7. How is the air different in the mountains and in the desert?
8. In what kinds of places is the air the dirtiest? In what kinds of places is it the cleanest?
9. What do we mean by "climate change"? What might be some causes of it?

Natural events that add things to the air

10. How does a volcano affect air quality?
11. What happens to the air when there is a forest fire?
12. How can ocean waves play a part in polluting the air we breathe?

Oral Presentation

You will often be asked to conduct research when you are a student. In this section, you will work with a partner and conduct a survey to find out what other people think about global warming. Then you and your partner will present the results of your survey to the class.

BEFORE THE PRESENTATION

1 Conduct a survey

Conducting a survey is a good way to get ideas about a topic from other people. The new ideas will help you think and talk about the topic with greater understanding. It is also a good opportunity to practice your speaking and listening skills.

A Work with a partner. Practice asking and answering each question below in preparation for your survey.

	What do you think is causing global warming?	What are some effects of global warming?	What can people do to slow global warming?
Interviewee #1			
Interviewee #2			
Interviewee #3			
Interviewee #4			
Interviewee #5			

B Survey five people outside of your class (your partner should survey five different people, for a total of 10 interviewees). Remember to ask each person politely if they will participate in your survey.

Excuse me, I am doing a survey for a class project. Do you have a few minutes to answer some questions about global warming?

You should also thank each person at the end of your survey.

Thank you very much for your time. / Thank you for answering my questions.

2 Compile your results

A After completing your surveys, work with a partner to compile (put together) your results. Summarize all 10 interviewees' responses and think about how you will explain your results to the class. Also prepare to explain your own opinion about the topic. Use some of the following expressions.

According to our survey, people think global warming is caused by . . .

Our interviewees said that some effects of global warming are . . .

Some suggestions for slowing global warming are . . .

I agree / disagree with some of our interviewees' opinions. For example, . . .

B Prepare a visual aid for your presentation. This could be a poster, a graph, or a chart, or simply a list of your survey results. Make your visual aid large enough to be seen by all members of your class. Remember that an effective visual aid helps communicate information clearly to your audience.

1 Use elements of good voice control

In order to be an effective speaker, you must be able to control your voice. In Unit 1, you learned about two elements of voice control: fluency and pace. Two more important elements of voice control are **volume** and **intonation**.

Volume refers to the loudness of your voice. When you give an oral presentation, it is important to speak loud enough for everyone in the room to hear your voice clearly. Remember to speak louder than you do normally in daily conversations. Focus on the people in the very back of the room – try to speak loud enough for them to hear you.

Intonation is the change in the pitch of words and sentences. It is sometimes described as the rise and fall of your voice when speaking. English speakers use a lot of intonation, so practice varying the rise and fall of your voice when you give your presentation. If you do not use intonation, your speech will sound flat and your audience may feel bored.

2 Transition to your partner

As you learned in Unit 2, when you work with a partner it is important to decide in advance which part of the speech each of you will present to the class. You and your partner should both speak for about the same amount of time. Practice transitioning smoothly from one speaker to the other using some of these expressions.

I would like to start by telling you about the causes of global warming. Then, _____ will tell you about its effects.

That summarizes the effects of global warming. Now, _____ will explain some ways people can help slow global warming.

We learned a lot of interesting information from our interviewees. To conclude our presentation, _____ and I would like to share our own opinions about global warming.

Give and receive peer feedback

When you give feedback about your classmates' presentations, you may feel uncomfortable saying anything negative. However, feedback should point out the speaker's strengths as well as areas they can improve. Remember that the purpose of peer feedback is to help your classmates improve their speaking skills.

For this presentation, you will fill out the peer feedback form below for each of your classmates' presentations. Your comments should be honest, constructive and respectful.

You will also receive feedback from your classmates about your speech. Look over their comments carefully and think about how you can improve your next presentation.

Peer Feedback Form
Evaluator (your name): _____
(Circle one answer: 1 = needs improvement   2 = good   3 = excellent)
Presentation content (organized, interesting)   1   2   3
Visual aid (neat, clear)   1   2   3
Teamwork (equal speaking time, smooth transitions)   1   2   3

Speaker 1 _____	Speaker 2 _____
Fluency 1 2 3	Fluency 1 2 3
Pace 1 2 3	Pace 1 2 3
Volume 1 2 3	Volume 1 2 3
Intonation 1 2 3	Intonation 1 2 3

COMMENTS:

Unit 4
Life on Earth

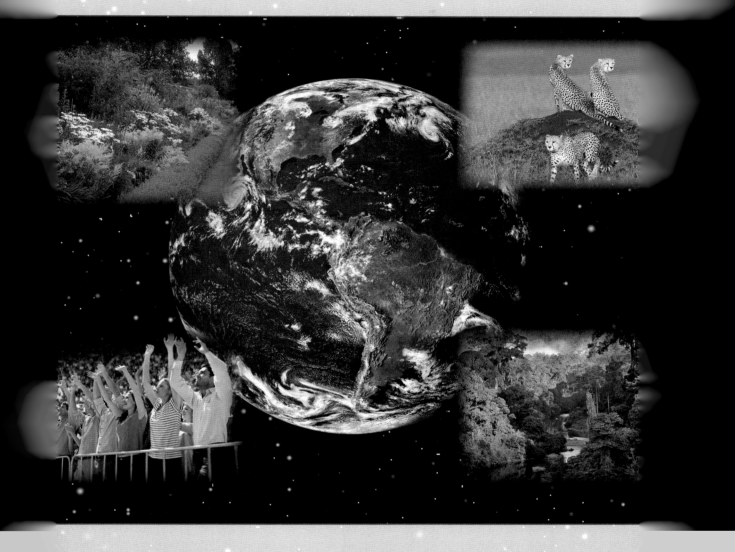

This unit is about Earth's biosphere. *Biosphere* refers to all of the living things on Earth: plants, animals, and humans. In Chapter 7, you are going to hear interviews with people who are interested in different kinds of plants and animals. The lecture explains the processes that all living things have in common. Chapter 8 focuses on one form of life in the biosphere: humans. In the interviews, two people talk about the human body and how to keep it strong and healthy. The lecture takes a look at different systems in the human body.

Contents

In Unit 4, you will listen to and speak about the following topics.

Chapter 7 Plants and Animals	Chapter 8 Humans
Interview 1 A Green Thumb **Interview 2** The Galapagos Islands **Lecture** What Is a Living Thing?	**Interview 1** Running Track **Interview 2** Eat to Live, Don't Live to Eat **Lecture** Systems of the Human Body

Skills

In Unit 4, you will practice the following skills.

L Listening Skills

Listening for specific information
Listening for examples
Listening to directions
Listening for main ideas
Listening for expressions of time order
Listening for expressions of contrast

S Speaking Skills

Personalizing the topic
Building background knowledge
Examining graphic material
Thinking critically about the topic
Conducting an interview
Applying what you have learned
Conducting a survey
Considering related information
Sharing your opinion

V Vocabulary Skills

Reading and thinking about the topic
Examining vocabulary in context
Previewing the topic
Guessing vocabulary from context
Building background knowledge and
   vocabulary

N Note Taking Skills

Checking your notes
Organizing your notes in a chart
Taking notes in a flowchart
Evaluating your own note taking

Learning Outcomes

Prepare and **deliver** an oral presentation about a living thing in Earth's biosphere

Chapter 7
Plants and Animals

Look at the photograph and answer the questions with a partner.

1. What plants and animals do you see in the picture? How many can you name?

2. What do all of these plants and animals have in common?

1 Getting Started

In this section, you are going to read about the different forms of life on Earth and some of the things that all living things have in common. You will also listen to information about some unusual plants and animals that live on our planet.

1 Reading and thinking about the topic Ⓥ Ⓢ

A Read the following passage.

Many different kinds of organisms, or living things, live on Earth. Scientists have not been able to count all of them, but so far, they have identified more than 2 million species (types) of living things. This number includes more than 300,000 species of plants and more than 1.8 million species of animals.

When you think about the plants and animals on Earth – for example, trees, flowers, grasses, insects, fish, birds, and mammals – it may seem at first that they have nothing in common. However, all plants and animals share some characteristics: They move, they grow, and they use food and water to make energy. All plants and animals react to their environment, and they can all reproduce themselves. Finally, all organisms are interconnected. This means that they need each other to continue living. If we lose even one plant or animal species, it affects the balance of life on Earth.

B Answer the following questions according to the information in the passage.

1. Have scientists identified more kinds of plants or more kinds of animals on Earth? How many more?
2. Name six ways that plants and animals are similar.

C Read the following questions and share your answers with a partner.

1. Describe the plants that live in the area where you grew up.
2. Describe the animals that live in the area where you grew up.

2 Listening for specific information Ⓛ

A Look at the pictures below. Write the name of each plant or animal under the correct picture.

bamboo, blue whale, giant sequoia tree, Goliath beetle, platypus, Venus flytrap

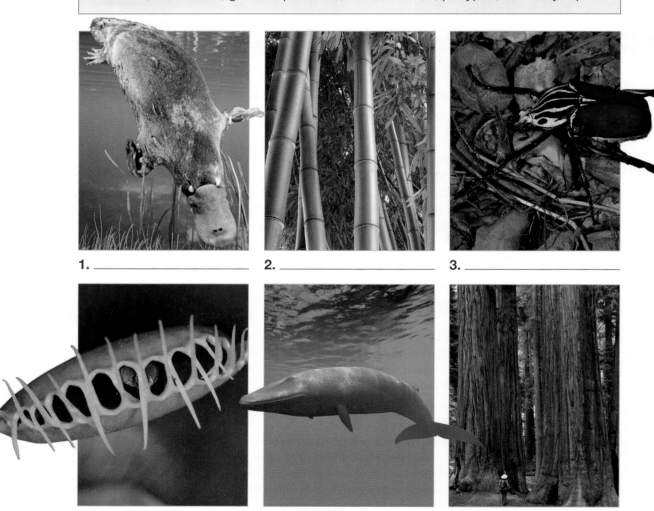

1. _____

2. _____

3. _____

4. _____

5. _____

6. _____

B With a partner, discuss what you know about each plant and animal in Step A.

◀» **C** Look at the chart below. Listen and complete the missing information.

Organism	Interesting facts	Habitat (where it lives)
1. blue whale	largest animal in the world	deep oceans
2. Venus flytrap	eats meat; catches insects	
3. platypus	has bill and webbed feet like duck, but has wide, flat tail	
4. giant sequoia tree		
5. Goliath beetle		
6.		

◀» **D** Listen again and check your answers to Step C. Add any other interesting information you hear about each organism.

2 Real-Life Voices

In this section, you are going to hear an interview with two people, Frank and Vickie, who love plants and gardening. Then you will listen to Reggie, a wildlife volunteer, talk about a trip he took to the Galapagos Islands.

BEFORE THE INTERVIEWS

1 Personalizing the topic ⓢ

A Interview a classmate and ask the questions below. Take notes on your partner's answers.

    1. Have you ever had a pet? If so, describe your favorite pet.

    2. What is your favorite wild animal? Why do you like it?

    3. Does anyone in your family grow plants? If so, describe the plants.

    4. Describe two ways that you use plants.

B Work in a small group. Take turns telling the group your partner's answers.

2 Building background knowledge on the topic ⓢ

A A *symbiotic relationship* is a close relationship between two things. Many organisms form symbiotic relationships in nature. In a symbiotic relationship, the two living things benefit from each other in some way. Here are some examples.

Clownfish and sea anemone

Ostrich and zebra

Flower and honeybee

Plover and crocodile

B Work with a partner and discuss the photos in Step A. Guess how each organism benefits from the symbiotic relationship. Check your answers at the bottom of page 130.

C Think of another example of a symbiotic relationship between two plants, two animals, or an animal and a plant. Explain your example to your partner.

1 Examining vocabulary in context Ⓥ

The words in **bold** are given in the context in which you will hear them in the interview. Definitions follow.

> I enjoy growing **native** plants: *originally from the area in which they are found*
>
> I like to get off the **trail**: *path through the woods or countryside*
>
> So you like the **challenge** of finding and collecting the plants: *interesting task or problem*
>
> What **attracted you to** gardening: *made you like*
>
> I just kind of had a **knack** for it: *ability to do something easily and well*
>
> Now what I do is mostly **perennials**: *plants that live for three or more years*
>
> Oh, that **makes sense**: *is easy to understand*
>
> **Annuals** are the ones that die in the winter: *plants that grow and die within one year*
>
> You know the **expression** "having a green thumb": *well-known saying*
>
> . . . for me, it's very **calming**: *creating a sense of peacefulness*

2 Listening for specific information Ⓛ Ⓝ

A Look at the chart and notice the information you need to listen for in the interview with Frank and Vickie.

	Frank	Vickie
How he or she became interested in gardening	When he was a kid, everybody _____ .	When she was younger, everyone was trying to _____ .
Favorite kind of plant to grow now	He likes to grow _____ plants.	She likes to grow _____ , which are plants that come back year after year.
What he or she likes about plants and gardening	He likes the _____ of finding and collecting the plants.	It helps her forget _____ . It also makes her feel _____ to the earth.

🔊 **B** Listen to the interview and complete the chart with the information you hear.

C Work with a partner and compare your answers.

1 Examining vocabulary in context Ⓥ

The words in **bold** are given in the context in which you will hear them in the interview.
Definitions follow.

. . . the **diversity** of the wildlife: *variety; range of different kinds*

There's been a lot of environmental damage already, so the idea that it's an
untouched environment is wrong: *not changed by humans*

There used to be 13 subspecies . . . but now two are **extinct**: *no longer existing*

It shows a **lack** of understanding: *absence of something needed or desired*

Any **ecosystem** is so closely connected that even one small thing can change the
balance: *relationships among all the plants and animals in an area, and with the
environment they live in*

There's a tree that one kind of bird uses for food and **shelter**: *something that
provides cover or protection, as from the weather*

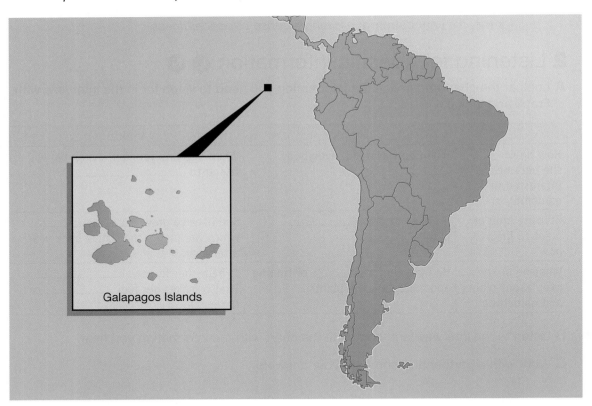

Galapagos Islands

2 Listening for examples 🅛

Speakers often use examples to help explain points or ideas. An example might be a story, a statistic, or a supporting detail. Understanding the example will help you understand the speaker's main idea. Some common phrases that introduce examples are:

for example   *for instance*   *like*   *such as*

A In his interview, Reggie gives an example to explain each of the statements below. As you listen, circle the phrase he uses to introduce each example.

1. You don't have to go far before you see wildlife. (*For example,* / *For instance,*)

2. . . . I saw a lot of birds. Many different kinds of birds, (*such as* / *like*)

3. There's been a lot of environmental damage already, so the idea that it's an untouched environment is wrong. (*Let me give you an example:* / *For example,*)

4. . . . any ecosystem is so closely connected that even one small thing can change the balance and destroy the system. (*For example,* / *For instance,*)

B Listen to the interview again. This time, draw lines from the phrases in Step A to the phrases below to form complete sentences.

a. blue-footed boobies, red-footed boobies, albatross . . . also pelicans, flamingos, and penguins.

b. there used to be 13 subspecies of Galapagos giant tortoises, but now two are extinct.

c. there's a tree that one kind of bird uses for food and shelter. If you cut down the tree, you lose the bird, too.

d. on the day I arrived . . . I saw Galapagos sea lions right away. I'd been there only 20 minutes and I saw sea lions.

C Compare your answers to Steps A and B with a partner.

Blue-footed boobies

1 Examining graphic material ⓢ

A Look at the chart below. It shows the numbers of threatened (in danger of extinction) species on Earth in 2000 and 2012.

Group of organisms	Number of threatened species in 2000	Number of threatened species in 2012
Mammals	1,130	1,140
Birds	1,183	1,313
Reptiles	296	802
Amphibians	146	1,931
Fish	752	2,041
Insects	555	776
Plants	5,611	9,193

Source: International Union for the Conservation of Nature and Natural Resources

B Discuss the following questions with a partner. Base your answers on the information in the chart as well as your own ideas.

1. Which group of organisms had the most threatened species in 2000? Which group had the most threatened species in 2012?
2. Which group had the greatest increase in threatened species between 2000 and 2012? Did any groups become less threatened by 2012? What do you think are some of the reasons for these changes?
3. What changes do you predict you will see in this chart in the future? Explain.
4. What information in the chart surprises you most? Why?

2 Thinking critically about the topic ⓢ

Work in a small group. Choose two of the following statements to discuss.
Explain why you agree or disagree with each statement.

1. All people should be vegetarians (people who do not eat meat or fish).
2. It is acceptable to use animals for medical research.
3. Space for humans to live is more important than space for plants to live.
4. Protecting Earth's biosphere should be the number one priority of the government right now.

3 In Your Own Voice

In this section, you are going to interview someone to learn more about native plants. After the interview, you will present your information to the class.

Conducting an interview Ⓢ

> An interview is a meeting with someone who has personal or expert knowledge about a topic. The person asking questions is the *interviewer*; the person answering the questions is the *interviewee*. Conducting interviews is a useful way for you to gather information about a topic.

A The purpose of this project is to learn about the native plants growing in your local area. Work with a partner to develop questions about the subjects listed below.

You want to know about . . .	So you could ask . . .
the interviewee's background.	*When did you become interested in plants?* *Why are you interested in plants?* *How did you learn about plants?*
native plants that grow in your local area.	
problems or dangers faced by local native plants.	
Your own ideas:	

B Make an appointment with your interviewee. Your interviewee can be anyone who is knowledgeable about plants, for example:

- someone who works at a farm, plant nursery, park, nature preserve, etc.
- an environmentalist
- a teacher who knows about plant life, selecting plants, or the natural environment
- someone whose hobby is gardening or collecting plants

Introduce yourself to your interviewee and explain the purpose of the interview. Be sure to ask politely for an appointment. You can use this model:

Hello. My name is _____ and I'm doing research about local native plants. May I ask you a few questions?

If the person agrees to be interviewed, you can say:

The interview will take about 15 minutes. When is a convenient time for you?

C Conduct your interview. Take good notes on your interviewee's answers. Be sure to thank him or her after the interview:

Thank you for your time.

D Organize your interview results and present them to the class. Remember to use signal words each time you introduce a new main idea. For example:

Today, I'm going to present the results of my interview about local native plants.

First, let me tell you about my interviewee. His / Her name is . . .

Next, I'll talk about some native plants that grow in our area . . .

Unfortunately, local native plants face some dangers . . .

Finally, I asked (name of interviewee) about . . .

Do you have any questions?

4 Academic Listening and Note Taking

In this section, you are going to hear and take notes on a two-part lecture by Dr. John Norris, a biologist. In his lecture, "What Is a Living Thing?" Dr. Norris will explain the seven processes that an organism must perform to be considered a living thing. He will also compare how plants and animals carry out these processes.

BEFORE THE LECTURE

1 Previewing the topic

> One way to preview a lecture topic is to study key vocabulary before you listen. This will increase your knowledge of the topic and will help you understand the lecture.

A In the lecture, you will hear about the seven life processes. With a partner, discuss the processes, which are listed below. Tell your partner what you think each word means. Circle any words you do not know.

excretion	reproduction	growth	respiration
movement	sensitivity	nutrition	

B Now study the roots and prefixes (word parts) below. Use this information to guess the meaning of the processes you do not know.

> *sensi*: feel *nutri*: feed *spire*: breathe
> *excret*: separate *re-*: again *produce*: make

C Use a dictionary to check the definitions of all seven life processes. Were your guesses correct?

2 Listening for expressions of contrast Ⓛ Ⓝ

> Lecturers often explain ideas by showing how one thing is different from another. Listen for signal words that indicate contrast, because they will help you understand the differences. The following signal words and expressions are often used to indicate how things are different from each other.
>
> | | | |
> |---|---|---|
> | *but* | *in contrast* | *unlike* |
> | *however* | *on the other hand* | *whereas* |

A Look at the incomplete sentences from the lecture below. Circle the expressions of contrast in each set of sentences.

1. Plants, for example, grow taller and wider throughout their lives. Animals start growing as soon as they are born. Unlike plants, however, . . .

   _____

   _____

2. I'm sure you can think of many examples of different kinds of animal movement. . . . Plants move, too, but . . .

   _____

   _____

3. Plants have a very special way of getting food – they make it themselves. . . . Animals, on the other hand, . . .

   _____

   _____

4. The process of respiration helps to change food into energy. Now, animals take in oxygen by breathing in air, whereas plants . . .

   _____

   _____

5. During reproduction, plants and animals make more of their own kind. Animals have babies or lay eggs. In contrast, most plants . . .

   _____

   _____

B Discuss the sentences in Step A with a partner. Predict what the lecturer may say to complete each sentence.

C Watch or listen to the excerpts from Dr. Norris's lecture. As you listen, take notes on the lines above about the contrasting information he presents about plants and animals. Then show your answers to a partner and compare notes.

1 Guessing vocabulary from context Ⓥ

A The following sentences are from Part 1 of the lecture. Work with a partner. Using the context and your knowledge of related words, take turns trying to guess the meanings of the words in **bold**.

_____ **1.** When scientists want to check if something is living or nonliving, they look for seven life **processes**.

_____ **2.** I'll start with two life processes that are easy to **observe** and understand.

_____ **3.** Plants move their **roots** down into the earth and their leaves up to the sky.

_____ **4.** An interesting **similarity** between plants and animals is that they all move for the same reasons . . .

_____ **5.** . . . to get food, to find a safe place to live, and to **escape** from danger.

_____ **6.** Living things **notice** their environment and respond to changes in their environment.

_____ **7.** Animals take in information about their environment by using their **senses**.

B Work with your partner. Match the terms in **bold** in the sentences in Step A with their definitions below. Check your answers in a dictionary if necessary.

a. the part of a plant that grows under the ground

b. sameness; something in common

c. to watch over a period of time in order to study or understand something

d. ability to hear, touch, see, taste, and smell

e. become aware of; see

f. get away from something bad or threatening

g. a series of steps or changes

2 Checking your notes N L

After a lecture, review your notes as soon as possible and check for incomplete information. If you find any errors, correct your notes.

A Look at a student's notes from Part 1 of Dr. Norris's lecture. Some of the information is incorrect. Circle the information you think is wrong.

Life process	Plants	Animals
Growth (size↑)	Grow taller and wider t/out life	Start at birth Stop growing when they die
Movement	– move roots ↓ e, stems + lvs ↑ to sky – flwrs open + close – faster than anim mvmt	Ex walk, fly, swim, etc.
	Both P + A move to get food, safe place to live, esc from danger	
Sensitivity (notice envir; respond to changes in envir)	– more senses than anim – react to stimuli, ex H_2O, light – sunflwr follows moon	– Senses: see, hear, smell, taste, talk – Use to get info + react to envir

🔊 **B** Now watch or listen to Part 1 of the lecture. Cross out or correct any inaccurate
📹 information in Step A.

C Show your corrections to a partner. Discuss any differences in your notes.

1 Guessing vocabulary from context Ⓥ

A The items below are from Part 2 of the lecture. Work with a partner. Using the context
and your knowledge of related words, take turns trying to guess the meanings of the
words in **bold**.

_____ 1 They **combine** the carbon dioxide with water and sunlight to make food.

_____ 2. This food is **stored** inside the plant and used when the plant needs energy.

_____ 3. During respiration and the other life actions, plants and animals create **waste**
materials.

_____ 4. Animals move waste out of their bodies in their breath, sweat, urine, and
excrement.

_____ 5. During reproduction, plants and animals make more of their own **kind**.

_____ 6. Usually we can easily **identify** something as living . . .

B Work with your partner. Match the terms in **bold** in the sentences in Step A with their
definitions below. Check your answers in a dictionary if necessary.

a. type; sort

b. water and nutrients that are used and pass through the body

c. to label or name something

d. used; left over

e. mix together

f. put or held somewhere for use in the future

2 Organizing your notes in a chart Ⓝ Ⓛ

A Copy the following chart and partial notes from Part 2 of Dr. Norris's lecture onto your own paper. Think about what kinds of information is missing from the chart.

Life process	Plants	Animals
Nutrition (getting food)	– CO_2 + H_2O + sunlight = food – Stored in plnt, used when plnt needs energy	– –
Respiration (food → energy using O_2)	–	–
Excretion (remove waste)	– – –	– breath, sweat, urine, excrement
Reproduction (make more of own kind, nec to cont species)	–	– –

🔊 **B** Now watch or listen to Part 2 of the lecture and complete the chart in Step A.

📹 **C** Review your notes. Correct any mistakes and then compare your notes with a partner.

Applying what you have learned Ⓢ

A All living organisms go through the seven life processes. Natural things that do not go through all seven processes are not considered living organisms. Work with a partner and complete the checklist below for *sunflower* and *fire*. Decide whether both are living organisms.

	1. Automobile	2. Sunflower	3. Fire	4. _____
Movement	✓			
Growth	✗			
Sensitivity	✓			
Nutrition	✓			
Respiration	✗			
Excretion	✓			
Reproduction	✗			
Living?	Y /Ⓝ	Y / N	Y / N	Y / N

B For column 4, think of your own idea and write it in the blank. Then fill in the checklist. Is it living or nonliving?

C Now read the list of actions below. Which life process(es) are going on in each one? Write down all possible answers.

1. A hermit crab becomes too big for its shell. It leaves and moves into a larger one.

_____

2. A plant in a dry climate sends roots deep into the soil, looking for water. When it finds a water source, it draws the water up through its roots.

_____

3. During a marathon, a runner begins to breathe hard. He also sweats a lot.

_____

4. At night, a cat's eyes open wide so that it can see better in the dark. It catches a mouse and eats it.

_____

D Discuss your answers to Steps A, B, and C with another pair of students. Discuss any differences you find in your answers.

Chapter 8
Humans

Look at the photographs and answer the questions with a partner.

1. What are the people doing in each picture?

2. How do these activities help their bodies?

1 Getting Started

In this section, you are going to read and talk about the human body. You will also perform some simple physical tasks to help you learn more about your own body.

1 Reading and thinking about the topic Ⓥ Ⓢ

A Read the following passage.

Of all the organisms on Earth, the one we all know best is the one we see in the mirror every day. But humans aren't especially unique. We are just one of the millions of different species on Earth. Like all living things, we are made of cells. We need food, water, and energy to survive; and we move, grow, reproduce, and go through all the other processes of life.

The human body has different systems to carry out its life processes. Each system has a separate function. For example, one system helps us process food, another helps us breathe, and a third helps us move. At the same time, the systems depend on each other; if even one system stops working, the others fail, too. It is important for us to take care of our bodies so that all of our systems stay strong and healthy.

B Answer the following questions according to the information in the passage.

 1. Which three systems are mentioned in the passage? Say what you know about those three systems.

 2. How does your environment make it easy or difficult for you to eat, drink, breathe, and move?

C Read the following questions and share your answers with a partner.

 1. Tell your partner about a recent health problem you have had, for example, a broken bone or a time you were sick. What caused the problem? What did you do to get healthy again?

 2. Think of the healthiest person you know. What does that person do to stay healthy? Describe him or her to your partner.

2 Listening to directions Ⓛ

🔊 **A** Listen and follow the speaker's directions.

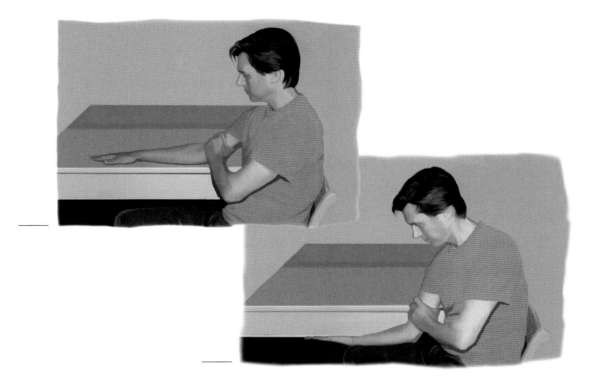

Task 1

How did your arm muscles change when you pushed down against the table? How did they change when you pushed up? Circle your answer.

 a. First, the front arm muscles flexed (became hard), and then the back arm muscles flexed.

 b. First, the back arm muscles flexed, and then the front arm muscles flexed.

 c. The front and back arm muscles flexed at the same time.

Task 2

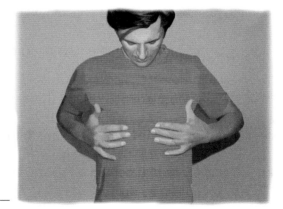

Number of breaths in 10 seconds

_____

Multiply by 6 = _____ per minute
(average breathing rate)

Task 3

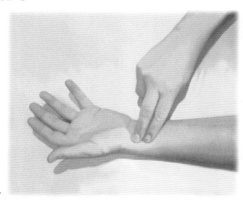

Number of beats in 10 seconds

_____

Multiply by 6 = _____ per minute
(average heartbeat rate)

B Compare your answers to the tasks in Step A with a partner.

C Read the descriptions of three body systems below. Work with your partner and decide which body system you observed in each task in Step A. Write the number on the line to the left of each picture.

1. The **cardiovascular system** is made up of blood, blood vessels, and the heart. Its main job is to bring nutrients and oxygen to all parts of the body.

2. The **muscular system** includes all the muscles of the body. Its main job is to work with the bones to enable the body to move.

3. The **respiratory system** is made up of the body's air passages and lungs. Its main job is to take oxygen into the body and move carbon dioxide out of the body.

2 Real-Life Voices

In this section, you are going to hear two people talk about staying healthy. First, Becca will talk about the benefits of different kinds of exercise. Then Louise will explain the importance of good nutrition.

BEFORE THE INTERVIEWS

1 Personalizing the topic ⓢ

A Read each statement in the checklist below. Then check (✓) the box that shows how often you do each healthy action.

Healthy habits checklist	Every day	4–5 times a week	2–3 times a week	Less than once a week
I eat breakfast in the morning.				
I sleep for seven hours or more.				
I exercise for 30 minutes or more.				
I eat fruits and vegetables.				
I eat a variety of foods.				
I drink at least eight glasses of water.				
Total points in column				

B Record the points for your healthy habits and total each column:

Every day: Record 3 points in each box you checked.

4–5 times a week: Record 2 points in each box you checked.

2–3 times a week: Record 1 point in each box you checked.

Less than once a week: Sorry! You get 0 points for each box you checked.

Add up your total points and write your score here: _____

C Compare your answers to Steps A and B with a partner. What can you do to improve your score? Do you have any other healthy habits?

2 Building background knowledge on the topic ⓢ

A Work with a partner. Look at the list of ways physical exercise can benefit the human body. Add any other benefits you can think of to the list.

    a. improves the quality of your sleep

    b. makes your heart and lungs stronger

    c. makes your body more flexible

    d. makes your muscles stronger

    e. _____

    f. _____

    g. _____

B With a partner, look at the forms of exercise below. Match the benefits in Step A to each of the exercises. Some exercises may have more than one benefit.

1. _____ swimming

2. _____ weight training

3. _____ bicycling

4. _____ yoga

5. _____ push-ups

6. _____ jogging

C Look at the exercises in Step B again. Discuss these questions with your partner.

- Which form of exercise do you like best?
- Why do you like it?
- In what ways does it benefit your body?
- What other forms of exercise do you enjoy?
- What sports or forms of exercise do you think are most beneficial?

The words in **bold** are given in the context in which you will hear them in the interview. Definitions follow.

> I was on the **track and field** team in college: *a group of sports that involve running, jumping, and throwing objects*
>
> . . . to make your heart stronger and to make your whole cardiovascular system work more **efficiently**: *in the best way, without wasting energy or time*
>
> After that, we did **drills**: *repetition of an activity to practice and improve skills*
>
> You practice the drills over and over again until your body remembers the **positions**: *ways the body and its parts are held or placed*
>
> The coach would have us . . . go right back into **sprinting** for another minute: *running very fast for a short distance*
>
> . . . you're running at a slower **pace**: *speed or rate of movement, especially walking or running*
>
> . . . sprinting . . . is good for **strengthening** your muscles: *making stronger*

Listening for main ideas Ⓛ Ⓢ

A In the interview, Becca talks about her training as a college athlete. Read the list of topics below. Predict what you will hear about how each type of exercise benefits the body. Share your predictions with a partner.

1. weight lifting
2. cardiovascular training
3. three- to five-mile runs
4. drills
5. sprinting

B Now listen to the interview. Were your predictions correct?

C Look at the list of the physical benefits of exercise that Becca talks about below. Match them with the actions you checked in Step A. Write the number of the action on the line next to the benefit. NOTE: Some actions have more than one benefit.

_____ brings in more oxygen for the muscles

_____ helps the body remember the best positions for running

_____ builds up the lungs

_____ makes the heart stronger

_____ builds muscle strength

_____ helps you breathe better

D Compare your answers to Steps B and C with a partner.

1 Examining vocabulary in context ⓥ

The words in **bold** are given in the context in which you will hear them in the interview. Definitions follow.

You're a **registered dietician**: *a professional who teaches people how to eat a healthy diet and who gives dietary advice*

Why is good **nutrition** so important: *the process by which an organism takes in and uses food*

Those six **nutrients** are your body's basic needs: *substances that give the body nourishment; substances in foods that allow the body to function and be healthy*

I talk to my patients about fiber, because fiber can help lower your **cholesterol**: *a waxy, fatlike substance in the cells of our bodies*

"Bad" cholesterol is what **clogs** our blood vessels: *blocks; fills*

That's the main role, to build and **repair** our muscles: *heal or fix*

People think fats are bad, but you need fats to help protect your **organs**: *groups of tissues forming a single structure in the body, such as a heart or a liver*

Those **go hand in hand**: *work together; cooperate; are closely related*

You need vitamin D to **absorb** the calcium from food: *take in or soak up*

2 Listening for specific information ⓛ ⓢ

A Read the title of Louise's interview. What do you think this expression means? Discuss your ideas with a partner.

B Louise talks about six nutrients in her interview. Work with your partner and discuss how each nutrient helps the body. Then match each benefit in the box on page 149 with the correct nutrient in the pictures below.

1. _____ Fiber   2. _____ Protein   3. _____ Carbohydrates

4. _____ Fat   5. _____ Calcium   6. _____ Vitamin D

Benefits

a. helps the body absorb calcium

b. main source of energy for the body

c. lowers the amount of cholesterol in the body

d. protects the organs and provides energy

e. builds strong bones

f. helps the body grow and builds muscles

◄» **C** Listen to the interview with Louise. Check your answers to Steps A and B.

AFTER THE INTERVIEWS

1 Conducting a survey ⓢ

A Survey the members of your class and ask them if they have ever been on a sports team. If they answer *Yes*, ask what kind of training the team does / did. Take notes as shown in the chart below. Try to find at least five different sports in your class.

Useful expressions: *Have you ever been on a sports team?*
What kind of training do / did you do with that team?

Sport	Kinds of training
Soccer	jogging, sprinting, stretching, passing + shooting drills, ball control

B Work in a small group. Compare the results of your survey. Which sports are most popular in your class?

2 Considering related information ⓢ

MyPlate is a set of nutrition guidelines based on a graphic of a plate and a glass. MyPlate was recently published by the United States Department of Agriculture. It replaces the older Food Pyramid. It will be used to educate people to help them eat a healthier diet. All food groups on MyPlate are important for good nutrition; however, people should eat more of some food groups than of others.

A Look at the graphic of the plate and glass below. Answer the questions that follow with a partner.

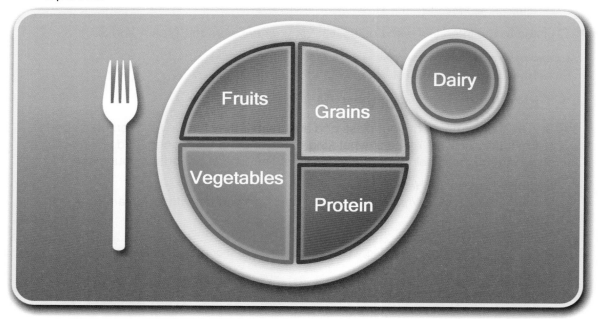

1. There are two food groups on the plate that each make up 30% of the recommended diet. Why are these food groups important?
2. What are the two food groups that each make up 20% of the recommended diet? Why do you think we should eat a little less of these foods than of the other two food groups?
3. Why do you think the group represented by the glass is not included in the groups on the plate?
4. Does this advice for a healthy diet surprise you? Why?

B Make a list of all the foods you ate yesterday, including drinks and snacks. Now compare your list with the MyPlate. Discuss the following questions with your partner.

1. Did you eat foods from all five food groups?
2. Did you eat enough of each kind of food?
3. Did you eat too much of any kind of food?
4. Did you eat foods that were not healthy at all – foods that were bad for you or had little or no nutritional value?
5. What changes could you make to your diet to help you meet the recommendations of the MyPlate?

3 In Your Own Voice

In this section you are going to read about a typical day in the life of a college student. You will identify unhealthy habits in his routine and give advice for improving his lifestyle.

Sharing your opinion Ⓢ

A Read the following information about Jim, a 19-year-old college student.

> Jim enjoys his college life. He is a good student; he attends all of his classes and does his homework. He also has a lot of friends and a busy social life, so in the evenings he goes out to parties or campus events. Recently, however, Jim has been feeling tired a lot. He has trouble staying awake in his classes, and he has gained 10 pounds.

B Look at the schedule below. It shows a typical day in Jim's life.

Jim's typical day

8:45	Wakes up.
9:30	Hurries to get to first class on time.
12:30	Buys lunch. Usually gets the student special: hamburger, soda, and chips.
1:30	Goes to class. Feels sleepy, so drinks coffee during class.
3:00	Goes to library to study. To keep his energy up, eats a candy bar.
5:00	Has another candy bar and a soda.
7:30	Has dinner, usually a hot meal like chicken, rice, and broccoli, with a soda.
8:30	Meets friends. Goes to a party, club, campus event, etc.
12:00	Comes home. Has a snack, such as chips and a soda. Uses computer to check e-mail and for messaging, blogging, etc.
2:00	Goes to bed.

C Jim wants to feel more energetic and lose weight. What advice would you give him? With a partner, think of at least five changes Jim could make to improve his health. Then share your advice with the class. Use the expressions below to help you.

I think Jim should . . .

Jim eats too much / too many . . .

Jim doesn't eat / drink enough . . .

Jim needs to . . . in order to . . .

D Are any of your daily habits similar to Jim's? How can you improve your own daily habits? Tell your partner.

4 Academic Listening and Note Taking

In this section, you are going to hear and take notes on a two-part lecture by Anthony Modesto, MD. In his lecture, "Systems of the Human Body," Dr. Modesto will describe three systems of the human body: the digestive system, the respiratory system, and the cardiovascular system. The first part of his lecture focuses on the digestive system.

BEFORE THE LECTURE

1 Building background knowledge on the topic Ⓥ Ⓢ

A Work with a partner. Can you identify the organs of the human body in this illustration? Use the words in the box to label each organ. Look up any words you do not know in your dictionary.

esophagus	large intestine	mouth	small intestine	trachea
heart	lungs	nose	stomach	veins and arteries

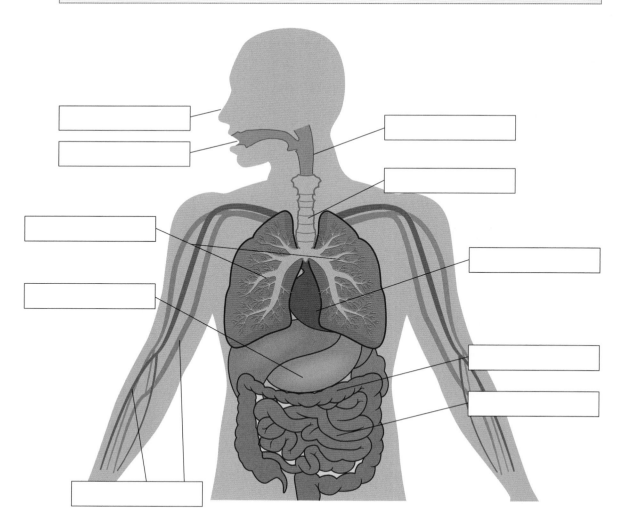

B Answer the following questions with a partner.

1. What do you think is the main function of each organ shown in Step A?
2. Each organ in Step A is part of the respiratory system, the digestive system, or the cardiovascular system. Which organs belong to which system?

2 Listening for expressions of time order Ⓛ Ⓝ

A lecturer often uses signal words to introduce steps in a process or a sequence of events. Noticing these expressions of time order will help you follow all of the steps and take accurate notes.

Some common words and expressions of time order:

first	*next*	*after ____ing, . . .*
second	*then*	*when X is over, . . .*
third	*after that*	*finally*

A The following sentences are from the lecture. Predict which words the lecturer will say. Use words from the box above and your own ideas to help you.

1. This phase can last for several hours, and _____ it's over, the food has become a thick soup.
2. From the stomach, the food _____ moves into the small intestine, where something very important happens.
3. _____ taking all of the nutrients out of the food, the body doesn't need the leftover food anymore.
4. When we breathe, air enters our body through our mouth and nose. _____ , it travels through an airway into our lungs.
5. _____ , the blood returns to the heart, ready to begin the cycle all over again.

B Watch or listen to the excerpts from the lecture and fill in the words you hear. Then work with a partner and compare answers.

1 Guessing vocabulary from context Ⓥ

A The following sentences are from Part 1 of the lecture. Work with a partner. Using the context and your knowledge of related words, take turns trying to guess the meanings of the words in **bold**.

_____ **1.** A body system is defined as a group of organs that work together to **carry out** a specific function.

_____ **2.** These systems carry out every **function** necessary for life.

_____ **3.** If even one of the systems **breaks down**, you'd be in big trouble.

_____ **4.** You wouldn't be able to **survive**.

_____ **5.** As your mouth moves and **chews** the food, the food becomes softer.

_____ **6.** When the pieces of food are small and soft enough to **swallow**, they travel from your mouth down to your stomach.

_____ **7.** In the stomach, powerful muscles **squeeze** the food and mix it together with chemicals.

_____ **8.** This **phase** can last for several hours, and when it's over, the food has become a thick soup.

_____ **9.** The body doesn't need the **leftover** food anymore.

B Work with your partner. Match the terms in **bold** in the sentences in Step A with their definitions below. Check your answers in a dictionary if necessary.

a. perform or do

b. remaining after the rest of something has been used

c. use muscles in your throat to move food or liquid from your mouth to your stomach

d. one period or stage in a series of events

e. purpose, role, or job

f. press or apply pressure all around something

g. fails

h. continue to be able to live

i. uses your teeth to break apart and crush food

2 Taking notes in a flowchart N L

A flowchart clearly shows the steps in a process. Organizing your notes in a flowchart will help you understand and remember the process better.

A Look at the partial notes from Part 1 of Dr. Modesto's lecture. Think about what kind of information is missing from the flowchart.

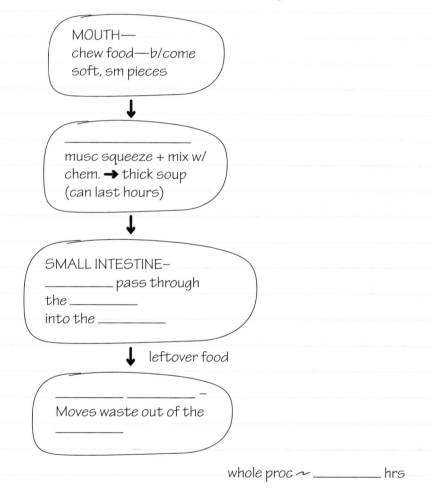

Digestive System
- body uses energy in food
- proc of bkng down food, releasing nutr into body = digestion

MOUTH—
chew food—b/come
soft, sm pieces

↓

_____
musc squeeze + mix w/
chem. ➜ thick soup
(can last hours)

↓

SMALL INTESTINE—
_____ pass through
the _____
into the _____

↓ leftover food

_____ _____ –
Moves waste out of the
_____

whole proc ~ _____ hrs

🔊 **B** Watch or listen to Part 1 of the lecture. Fill in the missing information in Step A.

👥 **C** Work with a partner and compare flowcharts.

1 Guessing vocabulary from context Ⓥ

A The following sentences are from Part 2 of the lecture. Work with a partner. Using the context and your knowledge of related words, take turns trying to guess the meanings of the words in **bold**.

_____ **1.** Next, it travels through an **airway** into our lungs.

_____ **2.** The air that enters our lungs **is rich with** oxygen.

_____ **3.** The cardiovascular system is made up of three things: our blood, our **blood vessels**, and the heart.

_____ **4.** The heart is the **source** of power in the cardiovascular system.

_____ **5.** As blood travels around the body, it gives oxygen and nutrients to each **cell**.

_____ **6.** When the oxygen in our blood has been **used up**, blood vessels carry it back to the heart.

_____ **7.** Well, that's a pretty simple **overview**, . . .

_____ **8.** . . . but I hope you can see how these three systems . . . work together to **maintain** life.

_____ **9.** The human body is truly **amazing**.

B Work with your partner. Match the terms in **bold** in the sentences in Step A with their definitions below. Check your answers in a dictionary if necessary.

a. keep something working or in good shape

b. structure like a pipe or tube in the body for air to flow through

c. wonderful, fantastic, unbelievable

d. structures that blood flows through as it moves through the body

e. has a lot of

f. place where something comes from

g. completely used; consumed

h. smallest unit of any living organism that is capable of functioning on its own

i. general description or summary

2 Taking notes in a flowchart Ⓝ Ⓛ Ⓢ

A Below is a flowchart from Part 2 of the lecture. Using the information in the flowchart, explain what happens in the body's respiratory system to a partner.

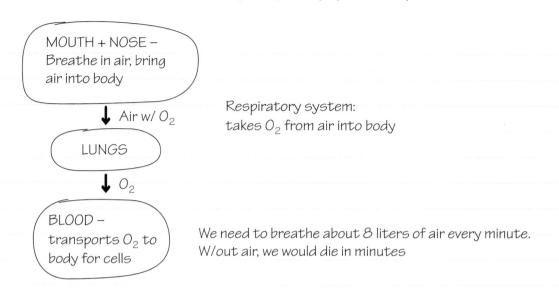

MOUTH + NOSE –
Breathe in air, bring
air into body

↓ Air w/ O_2

LUNGS

↓ O_2

BLOOD –
transports O_2 to
body for cells

Respiratory system:
takes O_2 from air into body

We need to breathe about 8 liters of air every minute.
W/out air, we would die in minutes

B Look at the notes below, which are from another section of the lecture. The note taker has listed information without making a flowchart. Think about the best way to organize this information in a flowchart.

Cardiovascular Syst. = blood, ♡, blood vessels

1. heart = source of power in card. system
2. blood leaves ♡ w/ lots of O_2
3. sm. intestine (dig. syst) – blood picks up nutrients
4. blood takes nutrients + O_2 to each cell in body
5. blood vessels carry blood back to ♡
6. ♡ pumps bld to lungs – picks up O_2
7. blood returns to ♡ – cycle begins again

🔊 **C** Now watch or listen to Part 2 of the lecture and the explanation of the processes
📹 shown the flowchart in Step A. Then use what you learned to make a flowchart using the notes in Step B.

D Work with a partner and compare your flowcharts.

Evaluating your own note taking Ⓝ

> You can improve your note-taking skills by regularly reviewing the techniques you have learned in this book and checking to see how well you have used them. After a lecture, look at your notes. Evaluate your strengths and weaknesses, and try to improve in your weaker areas.

A *Self-evaluation* means noticing the strong points and weak points in your own work. By working on your weak points, your note taking skills will improve. Read through the checklist below, along with your notes. Make check marks (✓) in the "Yes," "No," or "N/A" columns. Which skills did you use effectively? Which skills need more work?

Note taking self-evaluation			
Did you remember to . . . ?			
Before the lecture	Yes	No	N/A
Review background reading and other information about the topic			
Review key vocabulary that you are going to hear in the lecture			
During the lecture	Yes	No	N/A
Focus on the introduction			
Use telegraphic language			
Use symbols and abbreviations			
Notice signal words and phrases			
Identify key vocabulary			
Record numerical information			
Organize main ideas and supporting details in an appropriate format, such as an outline, a chart, bullets, brackets, etc.			
Use handouts, diagrams, and illustrations			
Focus on the conclusion			
After the lecture	Yes	No	N/A
Use strategies to fill in missing information			
Review and clarify your notes with your classmates			
Rewrite your lecture notes			

B Work in a group of three. Each person should summarize a different system of the body, based on your notes from the lecture. See the example expressions below for help in presenting the information.

The main job of the _____ system is to . . .

The _____ system is necessary for us to . . .

The _____ system is made up of . . .

_____ can be defined as . . .

_____ is / are . . .

Unit 4 Academic Vocabulary Review

This section reviews the vocabulary from Chapters 7 and 8. Some of the words that you needed to learn to understand the content of this unit are specific to its topics. Other words are more general. They appear across different academic fields and are extremely useful for all students to know. For a complete list of all the Academic Word List words in this book, see the Appendix on page 180.

A Read the sentences and fill in the blanks with a form of the word.

1. **cycle (n), cyclical (adj):**

   Blood moves in a _____ involving the heart, small intestine, and lungs.

2. **function (v), functional (adj):**

   One of his lungs isn't fully _____ because of a disease.

3. **identify (v), identification (n):**

   The _____ of threatened species is a priority for scientists.

4. **similarly (adv), similarity (n):**

   Animals need safe places to live; _____ , plants need areas that are protected.

5. **survive (v), survival (n):**

   Human activity is a threat to the _____ of many species.

6. **final (adj), finally (adv):**

   _____ , the leftover food passes out of the body as waste.

7. **react (v), reaction (n):**

   How did people _____ to the new nutrition guidelines?

8. **challenge (n), challenging (adj):**

   Adapting to new environments is a _____ process.

9. **diverse (adj), diversity (n):**

   The _____ of the Galapagos Islands is truly amazing.

10. **maintain (v), maintenance (n):**

    Our body systems work together to _____ life.

B Use the academic vocabulary from Step A to answer the following questions with a partner or as a class.

Plants and animals

1. How are plants and animals the same?
2. How are plants and animals different?
3. What should we do to protect species on the threatened species list?

The circulatory system

4. What is the circulatory system?
5. What is the route of blood through the body?
6. What happens in the small intestine?

Nutrition

7. What is the MyPlate?
8. What are some things you think most people could do to improve their diets?
9. What is "bad" cholesterol?

Exercise

10. How does exercise affect different systems of the human body?
11. What other benefits does exercise have?
12. What kinds of exercise would you recommend for young adults, middle-aged adults, and elderly adults?

Oral Presentation

A common project for students is giving an oral presentation in front of the entire class about a topic they have researched. In this section, you will choose one living thing in Earth's biosphere, research your topic, and share your information with the class in an individual oral presentation.

BEFORE THE PRESENTATION

1 Choose and research your topic

Your topic for this presentation is a living thing on Earth that has been very successful *or* a living thing that has become endangered. You may choose any type of plant or animal that interests you. If you want a challenge, you may choose humans as your presentation topic!

Brainstorm all of the information you know about your topic. You can use the brainstorming grid below to help you. Do some additional research on the Internet to learn more about your topic.

My topic is _____ . This is an example of an organism that is <u>very successful / endangered</u> on Earth.		
Description & habitat:	Interesting facts:	Reasons for success: (*or* reasons why it is endangered)

2 Prepare your presentation

A Organize your information in a PowerPoint presentation. Make a new slide for each main idea in your presentation. Do not put a lot of words on each slide; instead, use pictures and key words or phrases only. Use a 36-point or larger font to make the words easy for your audience to see.

B Practice your speech many times before your presentation date. Remember to focus on the elements of good speech that you learned in earlier units: fluency, pace, volume, and intonation.

DURING THE PRESENTATION

1 Outline your presentation

One effective presentation technique is outlining the main ideas of your speech during your introduction. This will help the audience understand the organization of your presentation and predict some of the information. Here is an example from a presentation about bamboo:

Good afternoon. Today, I would like to introduce an interesting plant, bamboo. In the first part of my presentation, I will describe what this plant looks like and where it lives. Then, I will tell you some surprising facts about bamboo. Finally, I will explain why this plant is a very successful organism on our planet.

2 Focus on body language

Your audience will notice your body language during your presentation, so be aware of it and use it to make your speech more effective.

Posture is the way you hold your body. Try to stand straight, but not too stiffly. Your posture can be relaxed, but be careful not to slouch your shoulders or lean on any furniture or the wall.

Facial expression is also very important. Sometimes when speakers are nervous, their facial expression looks serious or unfriendly. Remember to smile naturally at your audience and look interested. If your expression looks bored, your audience will feel the same way, too!

Some **movement** during your presentation can keep the audience's attention and help audience members focus on important points. Try taking a few steps forward or backward, or walking from one side of the screen to the other. However, be careful not to move too quickly or too often.

Self-evaluation

After you finish your presentation, think about how you did. Use the form below to evaluate yourself.

Self-Evaluation			
(Circle one:	1 = needs improvement	2 = satisfactory	3 = good)
Presentation content	1	2	3
Visual aid	1	2	3
Fluency	1	2	3
Pace	1	2	3
Volume	1	2	3
Intonation	1	2	3
Body language	1	2	3

Goal Setting: In which one or two areas do you most want to improve the next time you give a speech?

Map: The Continents

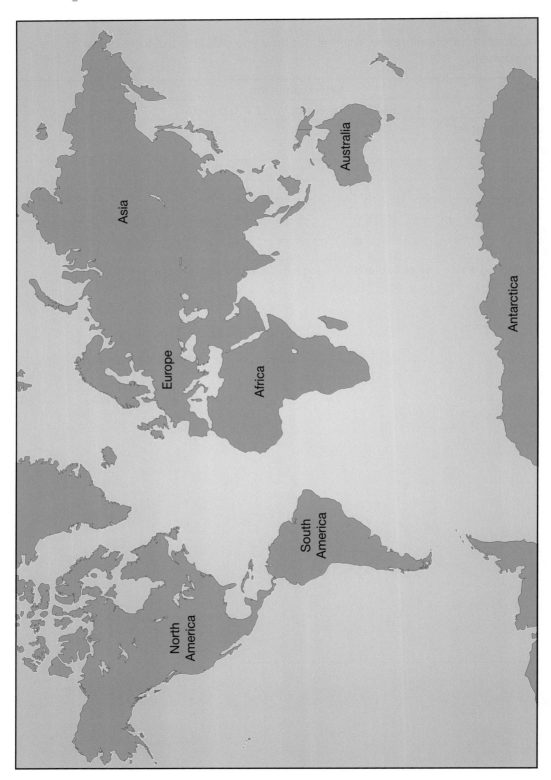

Evidence cards for "Sharing Ideas" on page 28

FOSSILS

Scientists have found fossils of the same kinds of plants and animals on different continents. For example, they have found fossils of the same kind of plant in Africa and Antarctica. Scientists have also found fossils of the same kind of animal in Africa and Asia. The evidence suggests that these continents were connected in the distant past.

ANIMALS

Today, we can find similar animals living on different continents. For example, we find marsupials only in Australia and North America. Because marsupials cannot travel across an ocean, scientists think North America and Australia were connected millions of years ago.

MOUNTAINS

Sometimes a mountain range that starts on one continent seems to continue on another continent. For example, if you pushed Africa and South America together, mountains on the west coast of Africa would line up with a similar mountain chain on the east coast of South America.

ROCKS AND MINERALS

Scientists have found the same kind of rocks on different continents. They have found the same kinds of minerals, including diamonds, in South Africa and Argentina, even though the two countries are nearly 5,000 miles apart.

Weights and Measures

The metric system is the system of measurement that all scientists use. It is also used by people in most countries of the world. In the United States, most non-scientists use the U.S. system. Some Web sites offer a free converter that you can use to convert measurements from one system to the other.

EXAMPLES OF THE METRIC SYSTEM AND ITS EQUIVALENTS IN THE U.S. SYSTEM

The metric system is based on the number 10, and it uses different prefixes for smaller and larger units. For example, a kilometer is 1,000 meters, a centimeter is one-hundredth of a meter (.01 meter), and a millimeter is one-thousandth of a meter (.001 meter).

Units of length

Metric system		U.S. system
1 millimeter (mm)		= 0.03937 inch
10 mm	= 1 centimeter (cm)	= 0.3937 inch
100 cm	= 1 meter (m)	= 39.37 inches
1000 m	= 1 kilometer (km)	= 0.6214 mile

Units of weight

Metric system		U.S. system
1 milligram (mg)		= 0.000035 ounce
1000 mg	= 1 gram (g)	= 0.035 ounce
1000 g	= 1 kilogram (kg)	= 2.205 pounds
1000 kg	= 1 metric ton	= 2,205 pounds

Units of liquid volume

Metric system	U.S. system
1 milliliter (ml)	= 0.03 fluid ounces
1000 ml = 1 liter (l)	= 33.81 fluid ounces
3.785 liters	= 1 gallon

EXAMPLES OF THE U.S. SYSTEM AND ITS EQUIVALENTS IN THE METRIC SYSTEM

Units of length

U.S. system		Metric system
1 inch (in)		= 2.54 centimeters
12 in	= 1 foot (ft)	= 0.3048 meters
3 ft	= 1 yard (yd)	= 0.9144 meters
1760 yd (5,280 ft)	= 1 mile (mi)	= 1.609 kilometers

Units of weight

U.S. system		Metric system
1 ounce (oz)		= 28.35 grams
16 oz	= 1 pound (lb)	= 0.4536 kilograms
2,000 lb	= 1 ton	= 907.18 kilograms

Units of liquid volume

U.S. system		Metric system
1 fluid ounce (fl oz)	= 0.007813 gallons (gal)	= 29.57 milliliters
32 fl oz	= 0.25 gal = 1 quart (qt)	= 0.9464 liters
128 fl oz	= 1 gal	= 3.785 liters

Temperature Scales

Scientists and most countries in the world use the Celsius, or centigrade, scale (°C) to measure temperature. In the United States, most people use the Fahrenheit scale (°F).

To convert temperatures from one scale to the other, use these formulas:

degrees Fahrenheit	= (°Celsius × 1.8) + 32
degrees Celsius	= (°Fahrenheit − 32) × 0.55

Lectures: Video script

Unit 1: Planet Earth
Chapter 1: The Physical Earth

Lecture:
"A Look Inside Planet Earth"
Before the Lecture:
Listening for main ideas in a lecture, page 11

Lecture topic.
Today, let's look inside Earth and discuss its internal structure.

First main idea.
But first, I want to give you some background information about our planet.

Second main idea.
Now, I'd like to discuss each of the three main layers of Earth. First, the crust. …There are two kinds of crust: oceanic and continental.

Third main idea.
Moving down from the crust, the next layer of Earth is called the mantle.

Fourth main idea.
Finally, continuing downward to the center of the planet, we come to the core. The core can be divided into two parts: an outer core and an inner core.

Lecture Part 1:
"Planet Earth: Background"
Listening for supporting details, page 14

When you think of the planet Earth, what do you think of? Probably the many natural features that you can see on Earth. For example, you probably think of mountains, forests, deserts, oceans, rivers and lakes, soil and rocks. All of these are important features on the surface of Earth. But have you ever thought about what's below Earth's surface? Today, let's look inside the planet Earth and discuss its internal structure.

But first, I want to give you some background information about our planet. As you know, there are eight planets in our solar system. Our planet, Earth, is the third planet from the sun. It is also the fifth largest planet in our solar system. How large is Earth? If we draw a line directly through the center of the planet, the distance from the North Pole to the South Pole is almost 13,000 kilometers.

Earth is made up of three main layers: the crust, the mantle, and the core. The crust is the outer layer of Earth. The mantle is the next layer, under the crust. The core is the last layer, at the center of Earth. Scientists can study these three layers by using seismic waves. Seismic waves are like waves of energy. Scientists send these waves of energy through the crust, the mantle, and the core, and watch carefully as the waves pass through the three layers. Seismic waves act differently as they pass through different kinds of materials, so scientists can learn important information about Earth's layers.

Lecture Part 2:
"Inside Our Planet Earth"
Listening for supporting details, page 16

Now, I'd like to discuss each of the three main layers of Earth. First, the crust. Earth's crust is what we see when we look at Earth's surface. If you imagine that Earth is a piece of fruit, the crust is like the skin of the fruit. Our planet's skin is made up of solid rock. There are two kinds of crust: oceanic and continental. Oceanic crust is all of the crust that is covered by Earth's oceans. Actually, most of Earth's crust is oceanic, because most of Earth's surface is covered with water.

Continental crust is the part of the crust that makes up Earth's land areas. Which do you think is thicker: oceanic crust, or continental crust? If you guessed continental crust, you're correct. Oceanic crust is only about 6 to 11 kilometers thick. Continental crust is thicker than oceanic crust, about 30 to 40 kilometers thick. And as I said, both kinds of crust are made up of solid rock.

Moving down from the crust, the next layer of Earth is called the mantle. This layer is much thicker than the crust; the mantle is about 2,900 kilometers deep. The upper part of the mantle is cool, solid rock, like the crust. But the further down you go into the mantle, the more the temperature increases. Because of the higher temperature, the lower part of the mantle is hot and soft.

Finally, continuing downward to the center of the planet, we come to the core. The core can be divided into two parts: an outer core and an inner core. The outer core is very, very hot. It is so hot, in fact, that the rocks here melt and become liquid. Think about that. Deep down below us, near the center of Earth, there is a layer of hot liquid rock!

At the very center of Earth there is a huge ball of very high pressure and high temperature material. This is called the inner core. Scientists believe the inner core is made up of two metals called iron and nickel. The pressure of Earth on this iron and nickel creates a lot of heat. Scientists guess that the temperature of the inner core may be as high as 4,000 degrees Celsius. This heat moves outward from the core and heats the planet from the inside.

Chapter 2: The Dynamic Earth

Lecture:
"Volcanoes"

Before the Lecture:
Focusing on the introduction, page 30

Today's lecture is going to be about volcanoes. I love volcanoes! I have loved volcanoes my whole life, ever since I was very young and I saw the volcano Kilauea in Hawaii. I didn't know it then, but I learned later that volcanoes make about 75 percent of all the rocks on the surface of Earth. When you look around and see rocks, remember that most of those rocks – 75% of them – come from volcanoes. So volcanoes are a really important topic when we talk about our natural world.

I'd like to start today's lecture by introducing the basic structure of a volcano – in other words, the different parts that every volcano has. Then I'll describe three basic types of volcanoes: shield volcanoes, composite volcanoes, and super volcanoes. For each basic type, I will also give you an example. Finally, we'll discuss some of the signs that volcanoes exhibit right before they are going to erupt. These are signs in the area

around a volcano that scientists can look for that warn that an eruption is about to happen. So let's get started.

Lecture Part 1:
"The Basic Structure of a Volcano"
Using telegraphic language, page 32

Today's lecture is going to be about volcanoes. I love volcanoes! I have loved volcanoes my whole life, ever since I was very young and I saw the volcano Kilauea in Hawaii. I didn't know it then, but I learned later that volcanoes make about 75 percent of all the rocks on the surface of Earth. When you look around and see rocks, remember that most of those rocks – 75% of them – come from volcanoes. So volcanoes are a really important topic when we talk about our natural world.

I'd like to start today's lecture by introducing the basic structure of a volcano – in other words, the different parts that every volcano has. Then I'll describe three basic types of volcanoes: shield volcanoes, composite volcanoes, and super volcanoes. For each basic type, I will also give you an example. Finally, we'll discuss some of the signs that volcanoes exhibit right before they are going to erupt. These are signs in the area around a volcano that scientists can look for that warn that an eruption is about to happen. So let's get started.

First, the basic structure of a volcano. Well, volcanoes are formed by hot, melted rock called magma. Magma comes from the Earth's mantle, which is a layer deep below Earth's surface. The upper mantle is from 80 to 150 kilometers below Earth's surface, and the temperatures here are so high that rocks start to melt and become magma. This magma flows through the mantle and pushes up against the solid rock above. Usually an eruption starts because an earthquake breaks the rock at the top of the mantle and creates an opening. The magma then rises through the opening in the solid rock and moves towards the surface of the Earth. Finally, the magma comes out of the opening in the crust, called a vent. Now, when magma flows onto the Earth's surface, we don't call it magma anymore. We call it lava. So, melted rock under the Earth's surface is called magma, but melted rock on top of the Earth's surface is called lava.

You probably think of a volcanic eruption as a big, loud explosion, right? But a volcano can erupt gently, as lava that flows along the surface of the Earth. Of course, a volcano can also erupt very powerfully, too. A powerful eruption can have clouds of ash and rock that rise thousands of meters into the sky.

Lecture Part 2:
"Types of Volcanoes"
Using telegraphic language, page 35

All right, now let's take a look at some of the different types of volcanoes. There are many different types of volcanoes, but today I will tell you about three basic types. The first kind of volcano is what we call a shield volcano. A shield volcano is usually very, very big. Lava flows out from its vent in gentle eruptions. The lava comes out of the vent gently and then flows along the surface of the Earth. The lava cools and becomes hard, forming a broad, circular shape. The shape kind of looks like a shield – broad and circular, with sloping sides – which is why these volcanoes are called "shield" volcanoes. An example of a shield volcano is Mauna Loa in Hawaii. It's the largest volcano on Earth. Mauna Loa starts on the sea floor and rises to over 9,000 meters.

Another type of volcano is the composite volcano. Composite volcanoes are smaller than shield volcanoes. The tallest composite volcanoes are only about 2,500 meters high. Composite volcanoes have both explosive and gentle eruptions. Often, the volcano will start with an explosive eruption and layers of ash and rock will pile up near the vent. Then a gentle eruption happens. The lava flows out

and covers the layers of ash from the first eruption, making a cone that has alternating layers of ash and lava. Do you know the meaning of composite? It means "made up of different parts." Composite volcanoes get their name because they are made up of different layers of ash and lava. A good example of a composite volcano is Mt. Fuji in Japan. Another example is Mt. St. Helens, which erupted in 1981.

The last type of volcano I'd like to talk about today is a super volcano. Super volcanoes are the biggest volcanoes and have the most explosive eruptions. They don't form a cone shape at all; instead, they leave a huge crater, or hole, in the ground. Eruptions from super volcanoes don't happen very often, but when a super volcano erupts, it causes widespread destruction that affects all life on Earth. Scientists believe that the largest super volcano was Toba. It erupted about 70 to 75 thousand years ago in Indonesia. Some scientists think that the Toba super volcano killed at least 60 percent of all people on Earth.

Pretty scary! But most volcanoes give some signs before they actually erupt, and today scientists are very good at noticing these signs before the eruptions. Some examples of warning signs are earthquakes and ground cracks. Another sign is when drinking water tastes different. Changes in the Earth sometimes affect the way water tastes, so this could be a sign that a volcano will erupt soon. Sometimes ice at the tops of volcanoes starts to melt. Volcanologists who study active volcanoes notice the melting ice and all of the other warning signs and can help in planning for and escaping from dangerous situations.

Unit 2: Water on Earth
Chapter 3: Earth's Water Supply

Lecture:
"Sources and Functions of Surface Water"
Before the Lecture:
Using symbols and abbreviations, page 55

1. Martha McDaniel: Anyone who has ever been to the ocean, or seen a picture of our planet taken from space, knows that there is plenty of water on Earth. In fact, most of the Earth's surface is covered in water.

2. However, almost all of that water is saltwater. In fact, 97 percent of the water on Earth is saltwater. That means only three percent of the water on Earth is freshwater.

3. Only three percent of the water on Earth is freshwater. But of that three percent, almost 75 percent is in the form of ice in the coldest parts of our planet. That means that only about 25 percent of the freshwater on Earth is in liquid form.

4. This small percentage – less than one percent of all the water on Earth – provides drinking water for every person on Earth, as well as for its plants and animals.

Lecture Part 1:
"Sources of Freshwater"
Using symbols and abbreviations, page 57

Anyone who has ever been to the ocean, or seen a picture of our planet taken from space, knows that there is plenty of water on Earth. In fact, most of the Earth's surface is covered in water. However, almost all of that water is saltwater. In fact, 97 percent of the water on Earth is saltwater. That means only three percent of the water on Earth is freshwater. That doesn't seem like very much freshwater for people to use and drink, does it? But wait! The amount we can use is even less than that.

As I said, only three percent of the water on Earth is freshwater. But of that three percent, almost 75 percent is in the form of ice in the coldest parts of our planet. That means that only about 25 percent of the freshwater on Earth is in liquid form. This small percentage – less than one percent of all the water on Earth – provides drinking water for every person on Earth, as well as for its plants and animals. Now that's amazing. Today I will talk about this amazing, precious resource, Earth's freshwater supply.

Where does freshwater come from? When rain or snow falls from the sky, much of the water sinks into the ground and becomes groundwater. But, if the water can't enter the ground, or if the ground is already full of water, then the water stays on the surface. This water starts to move over the surface, and as it flows, it cuts a path into the land. Over time, the path becomes deeper. Now that flow of water is called a stream. Streams are small, but if they combine, or come together, with other streams and become bigger, then we can call it a river. Sometimes, streams and rivers stop flowing and form a pond or lake. Other times, water keeps flowing across the land until it reaches the ocean.

Of course, freshwater is on the surface of Earth, too. It is in streams, rivers, ponds, and lakes. It helps people in many important ways. Rivers carry nutrients and spread them over the land as they flow. As a result, most land near rivers is rich and fertile, which means it is very good for growing plants. Many farms are located near rivers for this reason. Of course, farmers also need to give their crops freshwater every day to keep them healthy.

People also use freshwater for daily tasks, such as washing dishes and clothes, cleaning and bathing, and so on. Water is used in industry, for transportation, and just for playing and enjoyment. But the most important role of freshwater is to provide clean water for humans and animals to drink. Without freshwater, life on Earth could not exist as it does today.

Lecture Part 2:
"Threats to Earth's Freshwater Supply"
Using bullets and brackets to organize your notes, page 59

As you can see, people, plants, and animals need freshwater to survive. Unfortunately, there are many problems threatening Earth's freshwater supply today. Unsurprisingly, these problems are caused by humans. Land development for human purposes leads to the loss of our natural environment. I'm referring in particular to the construction of buildings, roads, and parking lots. When we cover the earth with concrete, the land can no longer absorb water. In other words, concrete prevents water and nutrients from entering the ground. Land development projects therefore affect Earth's freshwater supply in a negative way.

Pollution also affects our water supply. Pollution comes from many sources: factories, human waste, and fertilizers are just a few examples. Air pollution mixes with the rain, which falls to Earth and then enters the water supply. The trash that people drop on the street may end up in a stream or river. Farmers use fertilizers to help their crops grow, but then these chemicals seep into the ground and into the water. Some water supplies on Earth can no longer be used because they have become so polluted.

However, perhaps the biggest threat to our freshwater supply is overuse by humans. The total amount of water on Earth can never increase. In contrast, the number of people on Earth is increasing all the time. Every year, there are millions of new people on Earth, which means millions more people using and drinking water. An increase in population means a need for more food, which means more farming and more water for crops. People use more water every year, and this is causing problems all over the world. According to the World Water Council, more than one billion people do not have access to clean, safe water.

Water is our most important natural resource. No human could live more than a few days without water. Therefore, we must protect our water supply. People must learn not to waste water. All countries around the world need to cooperate in order to stop pollution and use water more carefully. Only by making changes now can we protect Earth's fresh, clean water for the future.

Chapter 4: Earth's Oceans

Lecture:
"One World Ocean"
Before the Lecture:
Listening for signal words, page 72

1. Some people say that there is one more ocean, called the Southern Ocean, down near the Antarctic continent. However, not all scientists agree that the Southern Ocean is a separate ocean basin.

2. The sun heats the seawater in this upper layer. Therefore, the surface layer is sometimes called the "sunlit zone."

3. The biggest difference between the surface layer and the middle layer is the temperature of the water. As I just said, the surface layer is relatively warm, with an average temperature of 17 degrees Celsius.

4. Sunlight becomes much weaker below the sunlit zone, so no plants can grow in the middle layer. Consequently, most of the animals living in this layer have to swim up to the surface layer to find food.

5. The animals that live here have to adapt to be able to live in this cold and dark environment. For example, many fish in the midnight zone do not have eyes.

Lecture Part 1:
"The World's Oceans"

Using handouts to help you take notes, page 74

The topic of our lecture today is Earth's oceans. The percentage of our planet that is covered by ocean water is actually very high. The planet is divided into two halves: the northern hemisphere, which is the top half of the Earth, and the southern hemisphere, or the bottom half. Eighty percent of the southern hemisphere is ocean. As for the top half, 61 percent of the northern hemisphere is ocean. Less than the southern hemisphere, but still quite a bit. The result is that 71 percent of the planet's surface is ocean and only 29 percent is land. Naturally all of the oceans are connected, so we can think of it as one world ocean, which is divided into four main ocean basins. These four basins are the Atlantic, the Pacific, the Indian, and the Arctic.

First we have the Atlantic Ocean, which stretches between Europe and Africa, and the Americas. Next, the Pacific Ocean, which is the largest and deepest ocean. The Pacific stretches between the Americas and Asia. Moving south, we have the Indian Ocean, which is easy to remember because it surrounds the country of India. And then, in the northern regions of our planet, we also have the Arctic Ocean, which is the smallest and shallowest ocean. Some people say that there is one more ocean, called the Southern Ocean, down near the Antarctic continent. However, not all scientists agree that the Southern Ocean is a separate ocean basin.

Again, the oceans are not actually separated. They are all connected, and water is constantly mixing and moving from one ocean to the other. This is why we can think of all our planet's oceans as one world ocean.

Earth's oceans are very, very deep. The average depth from the surface of the ocean down to the ocean floor is 4,200 meters. As one goes down from the surface, one finds a very interesting feature: the ocean has a layered structure. This is because seawater has different densities. Density has to do with "heaviness" – the quantity of matter in a particular space or area. In the next part of our lecture, I'd like to look in more detail at the ocean's layered structure.

Lecture Part 2:
"The Layers of the Ocean"

Using handouts to help you take notes, page 76

An interesting feature of the ocean is its layered structure. Let's talk about each of the three main layers, one by one. The first layer is called the surface layer. The surface layer is the top 100 to 200 meters of the ocean. The sun heats the seawater in this upper layer. Therefore, the surface layer is sometimes called the "sunlit zone." Its warmth and light permeate the surface layer, making it an ideal place for many forms of life. Most of the ocean's fish and other marine life are near the surface layer, where they can find a lot of algae and other plants to eat.

Beneath the first 200 meters or so of the ocean, the surface layer ends and the middle layer begins. The middle ocean layer goes down to about 1,000 meters in depth. The biggest difference between the surface layer and the middle layer is the temperature of the water. As I just said, the surface layer is relatively warm, with an average temperature of 17 degrees Celsius. By contrast, in the middle layer, the temperature drops very quickly. With every meter you go down, the temperature becomes colder and colder. By 1,000 meters, the average temperature of the ocean water is only 4 degrees Celsius. Sunlight becomes much weaker below the sunlit zone, so no plants can grow in the middle layer. Consequently, most of the animals living in this layer have to swim up to the surface layer to find food.

Below the middle layer of the ocean, there is the bottom layer, which is all the cold, dense water below 1,000 meters in depth. As you can imagine, there is no sunlight here at all, so the water is pitch black. As a result, this layer is sometimes called the "midnight zone." It has very cold, almost freezing temperatures. The animals that live here have to adapt to be able to live in this cold and dark environment. For example, many fish in the midnight zone do not have eyes. Some animals here make and give off their own light. Much of the ocean's bottom layer hasn't been studied yet, so scientists still don't know a lot about this deep environment.

So let's just review very quickly what we talked about today. We have four main oceans: the Atlantic, the Pacific, the Indian Ocean, and the Arctic Ocean. All of the oceans are connected, and as a result we can describe them as one world ocean. The oceans are deep and have a layered structure: there's a surface layer, a middle layer, and a bottom layer. There's much, much more to say about the ocean. It's the last unexplored region on Earth.

After the Lecture: Focusing on the conclusion,
page 77

So let's just review very quickly what we talked about today. We have four main oceans: the Atlantic, the Pacific, the Indian Ocean, and the Arctic Ocean. All of the oceans are connected, and as a result we can describe them as one world ocean. The oceans are deep and have a layered structure: there's a surface layer, a middle layer, and a bottom layer. There's much, much more to say about the ocean. It's the last unexplored region on Earth.

Unit 3: The Air Around Us
Chapter 5: Earth's Atmosphere

Lecture:
"What Is in the Air Out There?"
Before the Lecture:
Identifying key vocabulary in the lecture, page 97

1. The amount of water vapor in the air – in other words, the humidity level – is something I know you're all familiar with.

2. Have you ever thought about the idea of solids in the air? The term particulate matter is defined as any tiny pieces of solids that are small enough to float in the air.

3. Flowers, trees, plants – they release pollen, or a powder made by flowers, and other natural matter.

4. Humans also add particulate matter to the air. Because of human actions, there are some substances in the air that shouldn't be there, or there's too much of certain substances, and this is what we know as pollution.

Lecture Part 1:
"Humidity"
Organizing your notes in an outline, page 99

Take a deep breath. Have you ever thought about what you breathe in, every time you take a breath? We can't see it, we can't feel it, but air is all around us. Because we can't see air, we often think that air is empty. But air actually contains many different things. So today I'd like to talk about what's in the air out there.

You probably know that air around you is composed of a lot of different gases. The two main gases that make up the air are nitrogen and oxygen. Nitrogen makes up 78 percent and oxygen makes up 21 percent of the air we breathe. But there are also about 10 other gases that are in the air, in very small amounts. And even though we can't see or smell or taste these gases, we could not live without them.

The amount of water vapor in the air – in other words, the humidity level – is something I know you're all familiar with. If you hear on the news that today's humidity is 80 or 90 percent, that

means there's a lot of water vapor in the air. If you are outdoors and it is hot and humid, your clothes will probably feel sticky and you'll probably feel uncomfortable. But if you hear that today's humidity is 50 percent, that means there's a lot less water in the air. Fifty percent is comfortable for most people. Deserts and other dry places can have a humidity level of only 10 percent – not much water in the air at all. When you're outside in 10 percent humidity, your mouth will probably feel dry and you'll need to drink something soon.

Before we move on, let's talk about how water vapor gets into the air. The most obvious source is rain, snow, and other forms of liquid or solid water that falls from the clouds. Sometimes the rain or snow changes to vapor as it falls, and it stays in the air. But water vapor can also enter the air from sources on Earth: from oceans and rivers, from trees, plants, and even from the ground.

Lecture Part 2:
"Particulate Matter"
Organizing your notes in a chart, page 101

So far we've talked about gases and water vapor in the air. Have you ever thought about the idea of solids in the air? The term *particulate matter* is defined as any tiny pieces of solids that are small enough to float in the air. Now, these tiny pieces of matter are so small that they're carried in the air, and they're too light to fall to the ground. There are many different kinds of particulate matter; some are found in the air naturally, and others are human-made, that is, they're the result of human activity. I'd like to talk about a couple of different types of particulate matter. Let's start with particulate matter that occurs naturally.

When a volcano erupts, it shoots smoke and ash into the air. In the same way, a forest fire fills the air up with smoke. When the ocean waves crash against the shore, salt and sand fly into the air. Flowers, trees, plants – they release pollen, or a powder made by flowers, and other natural matter. Have you ever walked through a field and then started sneezing? That might be pollen in the air entering your nose. Dirt and dust from the environment may be picked up by the wind, then fly into our eyes and make them red and itchy. All of these are examples of naturally occurring particulate matter that is found in the air.

Humans also add particulate matter to the air. Because of human actions, there are some substances in the air that shouldn't be there, or there's too much of certain substances, and this is what we know as pollution. When humans burn wood for cooking and heating, or they burn plants or trees, they add particulate matter to the air. When humans cut down trees and take water from the land, it's easier for dirt and dust to be picked up and carried in the air. But the activity that creates the most pollution is the burning of coal and other fossil fuels. This means every time we use fuel to power a factory or run a car, pollution is added to the air we breathe.

When we breathe these particles in, they can hurt our eyes, our throats, and our noses, or cause more serious health problems. Let me just remind you, the next time you look around at all that "empty" air, there really is a lot out there.

Chapter 6: Weather and Climate

Lecture:
"Global Warming"

Before the Lecture:
Listening for numerical information, page 112

1. Since the beginning of Earth, about 4.6 billion years ago, there has been a mixture of gases surrounding the planet.

2. The atmosphere acts as a kind of shield and a filter. It reflects about thirty percent of the sun's energy back into space. Around 70 percent of it actually passes through the atmosphere. Of that 70 percent, much of it is absorbed by the clouds and air. Only half of the energy that passes through the atmosphere – about 35 percent – reaches the Earth's surface, which is warmed by the sun's energy.

3. This has led to a heating of Earth's surface. In the past 100 years, scientists have found an increase of one degree centigrade in the average temperature on Earth.

4. But unless we change the way we do things today – which means we must stop relying on fossil fuels for 80 percent of our energy supply – the amount of greenhouse gases will continue to increase, and temperatures will continue to go up.

Lecture Part 1:
"The Greenhouse Effect"
Copying a lecturer's illustrations, page 113

Well, the topic of my lecture today is global warming, but before I talk about that, I'm going to give you some background information about Earth's atmosphere. As you already know, the atmosphere is what we call the layer of gases that surrounds the planet. Since the beginning of Earth, about 4.6 billion years ago, there has been a mixture of gases surrounding the planet. Some of these gases are called "greenhouse gases." We call them greenhouse gases because they create a "greenhouse effect." That is, they make the atmosphere warmer, because they absorb heat from the sun.

Let's look more closely at the interactions that lead to the greenhouse effect. Energy from the sun is the force behind our climate systems. It approaches the Earth and enters the outer layers of our atmosphere. The atmosphere acts as a kind of shield and a filter. It reflects about thirty percent of the sun's energy back into space. Around 70 percent of it actually passes through the atmosphere. Of that 70 percent, much of it is absorbed by the clouds and air. Only half of the energy that passes through the atmosphere—about 35 percent--reaches the Earth's surface, which is warmed by the sun's energy. The Earth emits, or sends, this energy back towards the atmosphere. About ten percent of it leaks back into space, but most of the heat stays inside our atmosphere. This process helps to maintain global temperatures within certain limits. It's called a "greenhouse effect" because warmth is sealed inside, just like in a greenhouse.

We've always had greenhouse gases in our atmosphere, and we've always had a natural greenhouse effect on this planet. But what has happened in the past century or so is that human activities have added more greenhouse gases to the atmosphere. As a result, the greenhouse effect has become stronger. With more greenhouse gases in the atmosphere, more energy from Earth is absorbed. This has led to a heating of Earth's surface. In the past 100 years, scientists have found an increase of one degree centigrade in the average temperature on Earth. While there has been some debate, I think people have realized that the increased greenhouse effect is causing the problem of global warming.

Lecture Part 2:
"Effects of Global Warming"
Listening for cause and effect, page 115

An increase of one degree centigrade in Earth's temperature may not seem like a lot, but it actually causes many changes on our planet. What are the consequences of this increase in Earth's temperature? Today, I'd like to focus on two effects of global warming. The first is an increase in sea level. The sea level has risen over the past 100 years, between about 15 and 25 centimeters. It is rising now and will continue to rise in the future. Some of this rise is due to the heating of the ocean surface. When ocean waters warm, they expand, or get bigger, and so the sea level rises. Another cause is melting ice and snow. The melt water is entering the ocean and resulting in a rise in sea level.

Changes in the weather are another consequence of global warming. As Earth's temperatures continue to rise, some areas of the world will become wetter and some will become drier. Already many countries around the world are experiencing more and longer periods of drought, in other words, long periods of time without enough rain. In fact, the amount of land affected by drought has doubled since the 1970s. Another example of weather change is an increase in severe storm activity. Some scientists believe that if global warming continues, we will have more hurricanes. Hurricanes develop over warm oceans, and so the rise in ocean temperatures may cause more and perhaps stronger hurricanes.

Today I told you about just two effects of global warming: a rise in sea level, and changes in the weather. There are many other consequences of global warming. It's difficult to predict the future. But unless we change the way we do things today – which means we must stop relying on fossil fuels for 80 percent of our energy supply – the amount of greenhouse gases will continue to increase, and temperatures will continue to go up. Scientists predict that this century temperatures will rise to about three degrees centigrade higher than they are now. Sea levels are also likely to go higher, about 60 centimeters above their current level.

So, global warming is a real problem for all of us. It may be the most serious problem in our world today. And I think all of us, as individuals, must take action to solve this problem.

Unit 4: Life on Earth
Chapter 7: Plants and Animals

Lecture:
"What Is a Living Thing?"
Before the Lecture:
Listening for expressions of contrast, page 136

1. Plants, for example, grow taller and wider throughout their lives. Animals start growing as soon as they are born. Unlike plants, however, they usually stop growing when they become adults.

2. I'm sure you can think of many examples of different kinds of animal movement: walking, flying, swimming . . . Plants move, too, but not in the same way as animals.

3. Plants have a very special way of getting food – they make it themselves. To make their own food, plants take a gas called carbon dioxide out of the air. They combine the carbon dioxide with water and sunlight to make food. This food is stored inside the plant and used when the plant needs energy. Animals, on the other hand, cannot make their own food.

4. The process of respiration helps to change the food into energy. Now, animals take in oxygen by breathing in air, whereas plants take in oxygen through tiny holes in their leaves.

5. During reproduction, plants and animals make more of their own kind. Animals have babies or lay eggs. In contrast, most plants make seeds, which fall onto the soil and grow into new plants.

Lecture Part 1:
"Growth, Movement, and Sensitivity"
Checking your notes, page 139

Welcome to today's biology lecture, everyone. Biology is the study of all living things on our planet. But, what do we mean when we say "living thing"? What does it mean to be alive? Well, scientists have a very clear way to answer that question. When scientists want to check if something is living or nonliving, they look for seven life processes, or seven special actions that all living things must do. The seven life processes are movement, reproduction, sensitivity, growth, nutrition, respiration, and excretion. These seven actions are like a checklist. If something has all seven, it's a living thing. But if even one process is missing, then it cannot be called a living thing. As you can see, this checklist is very important to biologists, so in our lecture today, let's look at each life process in more detail.

I'll start with two life processes that are easy to observe and understand: growth and movement. All living things grow, which means that they increase in size. Plants, for example, grow taller and wider throughout their lives. Animals start growing as soon as they are born. Unlike plants, however, they usually stop growing when they become adults. All living things also move. I'm sure you can think of many examples of different kinds of animal movement: walking, flying, swimming . . . Plants move, too, but not in the same way as animals. Plants move their roots down into the earth and their leaves up towards the sky. Some flowers open in the morning and close at night. Of course, the movement of a plant is much slower than the movement of an animal. An interesting similarity between plants and animals is that they all move for the same reasons: to get food, to find a safe place to live, and to escape from danger.

Let's move on to the third life process on our checklist. This next process is called sensitivity. What that means is that living things notice their environment and respond to changes in their environment. Animals take in information about their environment by using their senses; in other words, they see, hear, smell, taste, and feel things around them. Plants also take in information about their environment. Although plants do not have as many senses as animals, they do notice changes in water and light. The sunflower got its name because it turns its flower to follow the sun all day long.

Lecture Part 2:
"Nutrition, Respiration, Excretion, and Reproduction"
Organizing your notes in a chart, page 140

The next two processes are nutrition and respiration. You've probably heard of nutrition before – that's the process of getting food, and all living things need food for energy. Plants have a very special way of getting food – they make it themselves. To make their own food, plants take a gas called carbon dioxide out of the air. They combine the carbon dioxide with water and sunlight to make food. This food is stored inside the plant and used when the plant needs energy. Animals, on the other hand, cannot make their own food. Because of this, they have to eat plants, or eat other animals that have eaten plants.

OK, so once food is inside a plant or animal, the next life process begins: respiration. And what is respiration? The process of respiration helps to change the food into energy. Now, animals take in oxygen by breathing in air, whereas plants take in oxygen through tiny holes in their leaves. In other words, we see that both plants and animals need and use oxygen to change food into energy inside their bodies. All living things need energy to support all the other life processes, so you can see why nutrition and respiration are so important.

During respiration and the other life actions, plants and animals create waste materials. These are extra materials that a living thing doesn't need, or want. If the waste isn't removed, it will become harmful. Plants pass waste through their leaves and through their roots. Animals move waste out of their bodies in their breath, sweat, urine, and excrement.

To quickly review, then, all living things grow, move, react, eat, respire, and excrete. All living things also grow old and finally die, so the final life process – reproduction – is necessary for life to continue into the future. During reproduction, plants and animals make more of their own kind. Animals have babies or lay eggs. In contrast, most plants make seeds, which fall onto the soil and grow into new plants.

All right, that's our checklist! For something to be called "living" it must show all seven life processes: movement, growth, sensitivity, nutrition, respiration, excretion, and reproduction. Usually we can easily identify something as living, but remember, it must meet all seven life processes. An automobile moves, an automobile can be sensitive, an automobile requires nutrition like gas, and it excretes smoke. But is it alive?

Chapter 8: Humans

Lecture:
"Systems of the Human Body"
Before the Lecture:
Listening for expressions of time order, page 153

1. This phase can last for several hours, and when it's over, the food has become a thick soup.

2. From the stomach, it then moves into the small intestine, where something very important happens.

3. After taking all of the nutrients out of the food, the body doesn't need the leftover food anymore.

4. When we breathe, air enters our body through our mouth and nose. Next, it travels through an airway into our lungs.

5. Finally, the blood returns to the heart, ready to begin the cycle all over again.

Lecture Part 1:
"The Digestive System"
Taking notes in a flowchart, page 155

Have you ever thought about all the things that happen inside your body? The human body, like all living organisms, has many different systems, which is the topic of our lecture today. A body system is defined as a group of organs that work together to carry out a very specific function. Humans have 11 different body systems! These systems carry out every function necessary for life. When your body is healthy, the systems work together very smoothly. But if even one of the systems breaks down, you'd be in big trouble. You wouldn't be able to survive.

Today, I'd like to focus on three of the 11 human body systems: the digestive system, the cardiovascular system, and the respiratory system. These three systems each have their own role in the body, but they also work together in very important ways. Together, they bring oxygen and nutrients to every part of the body. Of course, humans need oxygen and nutrients to live, so our digestive, cardiovascular, and respiratory systems are really important.

OK, where should I start? We all like to eat, so maybe I'll start with the digestive system. Our bodies use the energy in the food we eat to carry out all of our daily life functions. To get the energy from food, our body has to break it down and take the nutrients out of it. This process is called digestion.

Digestion begins as soon as you put food into your mouth. As your mouth moves and chews the food, it becomes softer and breaks apart into smaller pieces. When the pieces of food are small and soft enough to swallow, they travel from your mouth down to your stomach. There in the stomach, powerful muscles squeeze the food and mix it together with chemicals. This phase can last for several hours, and when it's over, the food has become a thick soup. From the stomach, it then moves into the small intestine, where something very important happens. Nutrients from the food pass through the intestine and move into the blood. Those nutrients have now become part of the cardiovascular system, which I'll talk about next.

We're not quite done with digestion – there's one more step. After taking all of the nutrients out of the food, the body doesn't need the leftover food anymore. This waste moves into the large intestine and finally, out of the body. The whole process of digestion, from mouth to large intestine, takes about 24 hours to complete.

Lecture Part 2:
"The Respiratory and Cardiovascular Systems"
Taking notes in a flowchart, page 157

Another important system is the respiratory system. Now, the job of this system is to bring oxygen from the air into the body. When we breathe, air enters our body through our mouth and nose. Next, it travels through an airway into our lungs. The air that enters our lungs is rich with oxygen. Inside the lungs, all of this oxygen passes into our blood. Like food, oxygen is necessary for life. Our body uses oxygen to carry out all of its life functions. We need to breathe about eight liters of air every minute to stay alive, and even more when we exercise. Without oxygen, we would die in just a few minutes.

By now, you've probably figured out that blood has many important roles in the human body. It brings nutrients from food, and oxygen from the air, to every part of our body. Blood is part of the cardiovascular system, and that's what I want to talk about next. The cardiovascular system is made up of three things: our blood, our blood vessels, and the heart. The heart is the source of power in the cardiovascular system. With every beat, the heart pushes blood in a cycle around the body – from the heart to the body, around the body, and finally back to the heart again.

When blood first leaves the heart, it's oxygenated, which just means that it's carrying a lot of oxygen. Vessels carry this oxygenated blood all over the body. One of the places the blood goes to is our small intestine. Do you remember what I said, what happens in the small intestine? That's where the blood picks up nutrients from food. As blood travels around the body, it gives oxygen and nutrients to each cell. When the oxygen in our blood has been used up, blood vessels carry it back to the heart. Then, it's pumped into the lungs to get fresh oxygen from the respiratory system. Finally, the blood returns to the heart, ready to begin the cycle all over again. The entire cycle – from heart to body and back to heart, to lungs and back to heart again – takes only 20 seconds.

Well, that's a pretty simple overview, but I hope you can see how these three systems – digestive, respiratory, and cardiovascular – work together to maintain life. The digestive system brings nutrients into the body. The respiratory system brings oxygen into the body. The cardiovascular system carries nutrients and oxygen to the cells. Today, we talked about only three of the body's 11 systems. When you consider that there are eight other equally important systems, you can see that the human body is truly amazing.

Appendix

Academic Word List vocabulary

access
adapt
adult
affect
affected
affecting
alternating
approach
area
category
challenge
challenging
chemical
consequence
consequently
constantly
construction
contrast
cooperate
core
couple
create
culture
cycle
cycling
debate
define
defined
definitely
diverse
diversity
dynamic
energy
environment
environmental
equipment
eroded
eroding

erosion
exhibit
expand
factor
feature
final
finally
focus
focused
function
global
identify
individual
instance
instruction
interaction
internal
job
labeled
layer
layered
lecture
lecturer
located
maintain
major
negative
obvious
obviously
occur
overlap
percent
percentage
period
phase
physical
physically
plus

predict
process
project
react
region
registered
relax
relaxed
release
rely
remove
require
resource
respond
response
role
similar
similarity
similarly
site
source
specific
stress
stressed
structure
survive
task
team
temporary
topic
transportation
trend
unique
volunteer
whereas
widespread

Skills Index

Credits

The authors and publishers acknowledge the following sources of copyright material and are grateful for the permissions granted. While every effort has been made, it has not always been possible to identify the sources of all the material used, or to trace all copyright holders. If any omissions are brought to our notice, we will be happy to include the appropriate acknowledgements on reprinting.

Illustration Credits

Page 4, 6, 9, 14, 15, 17, 20, 21, 27, 29, 36, 47, 51, 62, 74, 76, 89, 111, 130, 150, 152, 164: Kamae Design

Page 54, 94, 113, 148: Mark Duffin

Page 63, 66, 143, 144: Tom Croft

Page 109 (clockwise): Cartoonstock, www.cartoonstock.com; Cartoonstock, www.cartoonstock.com; Creators, www.creators.com. By permission of Mike Luckovich and Creators Syndicate, Inc.

Photography Credits

1 ©Jeremy Edwards/iStockphoto; 3 (*right*) ©101cats/iStockphoto; (*left*) ©Comstock Images/Thinkstock; 9 (*top left*) ©Andrew Zarivny/Shutterstock; (*top right*) ©Jan Rihak/iStockphoto; (*centre right*) ©prasit chansareekorn/Shutterstock; (*bottom left*) ©HAIBO BI/iStockphoto; (*bottom right*) ©iStockphoto/Thinkstock; 18 ©Martin Rietze/Westend61 GmbH/Alamy; 25 ©Sankei Archive via Getty Images/Getty Images; 33 ©IvanSabo/Shutterstock; 35 ©beboy/Shutterstock; 41 ©Wayne Lynch/All Canada Photos/Canopy/Corbis; 43 (*top left*) ©kristian sekulic/iStockphoto; (*top right*) ©Rick Rhay/iStockphoto; (*bottom*) ©Ulrich Mueller/iStockphoto; 45 (*clockwise from left to right*) ©Wayne Lynch/All Canada Photos/Canopy/Corbis; ©13/Ocean/Corbis; ©iStockphoto/Thinkstock; ©idiz/Shutterstock; ©Hemera Technologies/Photos.com/Thinkstock; ©Mlenny Photography/iStockphoto; 46 ©Wayne Lynch/All Canada Photos/Canopy/Corbis; 47 ©Wayne Lynch/All Canada Photos/Canopy/Corbis; 56 ©idiz/Shutterstock; 58 ©FORGET Patrick/SAGAPHOTO.COM/Alamy; 61 ©Sergey Nivens/Shutterstock; 62 ©Vlad61/Shutterstock; 64 (*left to right*) ©Arpad Benedek/iStockphoto; ©Anna Omelchenko/iStockphoto; 83 ©Zoonar/Thinkstock; 85 (*bottom left*) ©Dave & Les Jacobs/Blend Images/Corbis; (*top right*) ©pcruciatti/Shutterstock; 87 (*left to right*) ©Alija/iStockphoto; ©Alexandru Razvan Cofaru/iStockphoto; ©Ridofranz/iStockphoto; ©GIRAL/BSIP/BSIP SA/Alamy; 88 (*numbered in sequence from top left*) ©Vadim Petrakov/Shutterstock; ©ssuaphotos/Shutterstock; ©beboy/Shutterstock; ©smikeymikey1/Shutterstock; ©Stephen Shaver/AFP/Getty Images; ©Amanda Grandfield/iStockphoto; ©Dennis Hallinan/Alamy;

94 (*left to right*) ©Brett Gage/iStockphoto; ©iStockphoto/Thinkstock; ©cretolamna/Shutterstock; ©Skip ODonnell/iStockphoto; ©xiaoke ma/iStockphoto; 101 (*left to right*) ©iStockphoto/Thinkstock; ©Sander Kamp/iStockphoto; ©iStockphoto/Thinkstock; 102 (*left*) ©Kosorukov Dmitry/Shutterstock; (*right*) ©Arctic-Images/Getty Images; 105 (*left to right*) ©Mike Theiss/National Geographic/Getty Images; ©Paul Katz/Getty Images; ©Dennis K. Johnson/Getty Images; ©Michael Brown/Getty Images News/Getty Images; 114 ©Earl D. Walker/Shutterstock; 116 (*left*) ©Dr Juerg Alean/Science Source; (*right*) ©Dr Juerg Alean/Science Source; 120 ©Klaus Tiedge/Fancy/Corbis; 123 (*centre*) ©101cats/iStockphoto; (*bottom right*) ©Frans Lanting/Latitude/Corbis; (*bottom left*) ©Martin Barraud/OJO Images/Getty Images; (*top right*) ©Masterfile; (*top left*) ©Rod Edwards/Britain On View/Getty Images; 125 ©Glowimages/Canopy/Corbis; 126 (*numbered in sequence from top left*) ©Dave Watts/Alamy; ©iStockphoto/Thinkstock; ©David A. Northcott/Encyclopedia/Corbis; ©Marco Uliana/Shutterstock; ©Denis Scott/Comet/Corbis; ©Neale Clark/Robert Harding Picture Library/SuperStock; 127 ©Denis Scott/Comet/Corbis; 128 (*clockwise left to right*) ©Petr Bonek/Alamy; ©age fotostock/SuperStock; ©Juniors /SuperStock; ©Juniors /SuperStock; 131 ©Minden Pictures/Masterfile; 134 to 135 ©Pakhnyushcha/Shutterstock; 142 (*left*) ©Spotmatik/iStockphoto; (*right*) ©PhotoConcepts/iStockphoto; 146 (*clockwise left to right*) ©F1 ONLINE /SuperStock; ©mediaphotos/iStockphoto; ©Hero/Fancy/Corbis; ©Pavel Ilyukhin/Shutterstock; ©Michael Weber/imagebr imagebroker.net/SuperStock; ©Masterfile